Bach's Keyboard Music

Unlocking the Masters Series, No. 21

Series Editor: Robert Levine

Bach's Keyboard Music

Victor Lederer

AMADEUS PRESS

An Imprint of Hal Leonard Corporation
New York

Published in 2010 by Amadeus Press
An Imprint of Hal Leonard Corporation
7777 West Bluemound Road
Milwaukee, WI 53213

Trade Book Division Editorial Offices
19 West 21st Street, New York, NY 10010

Printed in the United States of America

Book design by Snow Creative Services

Library of Congress Cataloging-in-Publication Data

Lederer, Victor.
  Bach's keyboard music : a listener's guide / Victor Lederer.
     p. cm. — (Unlocking the masters series ; no. 21)
  Includes bibliographical references.
  ISBN 978-1-57467-182-7
  1. Bach, Johann Sebastian, 1685-1750. Keyboard music. 2. Keyboard instrument music—18th century—History and criticism. I. Title.
  ML410.B13L386 2010
  786.092—dc22
                                                            2010001079

www.amadeuspress.com

For Karen

Contents

Acknowledgments

Thanks to my family—Elaine, Paul, and Karen—for their love and support. Acuity, love of music, and patience stand high on the long list of my editor Bob Levine's virtues: thanks, as always, to him. And thanks to Bernie Rose for teaching me to play Bach.

Bach's Keyboard Music

Johann Sebastian Bach's music for keyboard falls easily into two broad categories: first, the works composed for the organ; then those he wrote for other keyboard instruments, chiefly the harpsichord and clavichord. Bach's organ music stands supreme in its field. His works for *Klavier*—the German word meaning "keyboard"—along with Beethoven's sonatas and the purely idiomatic works of Chopin and Debussy, represent the heart of the repertory of the professional pianist. (Works by Schumann appear often in recital and on recordings, but only a handful can be considered repertory staples.) And the influence of Bach on musicians of every stripe who followed is incalculable.

Most of Bach's output for harpsichord, clavichord, and piano, the last instrument developed in the composer's lifetime, and his organ music fall into well-defined categories. First come his systematic explorations of a musical idea, most notably the two volumes of *The Well-Tempered Clavier,* sometimes referred to by the reverent nickname "the Forty-eight." The importance in Western musical history of these two sets of preludes and fugues in all twenty-four keys seems impossible to over-rate, as most composers, performers, and students have studied them more or less closely and venerated them for their power, inventiveness, and expressive beauty. In these works Bach makes the potentially dry fugue sing, dance, and speak with eloquence and passion.

Then there are the wonderful suites of dance pieces published in sets of six. The most delicate and easy to play are the French Suites, whereas the English Suites and Partitas are larger in scale and more technically demanding. Of these last there are six published together as a set, and, a remarkable seventh, the French Overture, composed and published later. These deservedly popular works are much played and recorded. It may be that their origin in dance makes them more stylistically diverse and more high-spirited than "the Forty-eight." They are also probably easier for many listeners to get their ears around.

Bach composed some works in two and three parts, or voices—interchangeable words for thematic strands—as instructional tools. He must have been a demanding *Klavier* teacher, and his pupils, including his musically gifted children, clearly had to function at a high level, because the easiest of these are tricky, and the hardest very difficult indeed. Yet the Inventions, which is what the two-part pieces are called, and the Sinfonias (those in three parts) are utterly serious, offering no concessions toward the musically unsophisticated. They are "adult" in style, the composer having bestowed the same care and art on these short studies as he did on everything he wrote.

From early in the composer's career are the seven Toccatas, in which blazing displays of virtuosity alternate and contrast with more meditative passages. All are very difficult and the territory of accomplished performers only. Another great early work is the *Capriccio on the Departure of the Beloved Brother,* sweetly touching in its naive, old-fashioned style, and singular in Bach's output. Other magnificent one-offs include the Italian Concerto, a tribute to Italian compositional style, and the Chromatic Fantasy and Fugue, a brooding diptych that shows the composer at his most advanced, experimental, and passionate.

Music is a series of organized aural patterns. These patterns draw rhythm, melody, and harmony—the way tones relate to one another vertically—into compositions in which there is a clear sense of beginning and ending, and perhaps of conflict and resolution. (What troubles many listeners about much music of the twentieth century and after is the disruption of these predictable and comfortable patterns.) There is hardly a composer more pattern-driven than Bach: even the uninitiated can hear in the driving, throbbing impetus of his rhythm, his twisting melodies, and complex, dissonance-laden harmonies that the man is up to something, with a technique that seems to run on levels that may be striking, but intimidating, too, for the uninitiated listener. A numerologist and lover of puzzles, Bach invested his music with structures that underlie basic musical elements. As a man of faith, he imbued his works with praise of God in complex forms that continually surprise devotees who know his works note for note.

Bach is generally considered as the greatest master of counterpoint. Without having heard the term or knowing what it means, the casual or novice listener may perceive in Bach's music a tune that seems to be chasing itself, or is repeating in a systematic pattern; these are the sound of counterpoint, also known as *polyphony*, which means "many sounds." More a process than a form, counterpoint is a kind of linear weaving of note against note in a variety of procedures that range from strict, such as the canon, to freer, as in the fugue; we will revisit and learn more about both. But counterpoint, or polyphony, or part-writing, does indeed inform all Bach's music, forming crucial aspects, inside and out, of his works for keyboard.

Bach's focus on polyphony may be the most daunting aspect of his music for even the most willing novice. It seems undeniable that note-for-note writing has a particular sound, an intellectual rigor, a recondite quality that challenges some listeners. Counterpoint is, indeed, omnipresent in Bach's oeuvre, even in works that are neither canon nor fugue. It is always just below the surface, with parts tugging at one another with an inescapable linear, polyphonic pull. One simply must try to get the hang of it if all the glories of Bach's art are to be revealed. Fortunately, however, Bach's intellectual power is expressed with overwhelming energy, expressed by his rhythmic vigor and virtuosic joie de vivre. In spite of its rigorous structures, there is also a choreographic energy in Bach's music that everyone can hear and appreciate.

The two primary contrapuntal processes are the *canon* and the *fugue*. The first (the term *canon* means "rule" in Latin) is a more compact technique in which all parts copy the main voice literally. This may sound like sure path to monotony; perhaps with "Row, row, row your boat" and "Three blind mice," the examples of well-known canons invariably cited, it may be so. But composers have plenty of ways to vary the rigid pattern, including playing the parts backward or upside down, reversing their directions, as well as laying them out in notes that are longer and shorter, among other formal variations. Like every skilled composer (and as a lover of puzzles) Bach enjoyed devising ways to make the tight canonic process do the unexpected, and there can be no doubt as to his success. Every third of the *Goldberg Variations* is a canon, and in addition to their structural function, each is powerfully expressive and musically interesting.

The term *fugue* derives from the Latin *fuga,* or "flight"—*fugitive* has the same root. It is a kind of musical chase in which a theme is stated and then reiterated by each successive voice as it enters. Fugues are therefore conceived in a finite number of voices, from two to six. There are connective episodes, and there may be a second theme, called a countersubject. Two entries of the subject close together are called a *stretto*; these generally serve to intensify emotion. None of this necessarily makes a difference in readers' lives or listening, and few really need to trouble themselves about any of it. But they are a key to Bach's compositional technique, and of course performers do need at least a rough grasp of them. These are the most basic terms of counterpoint, which may help when listening to some of the selections on the compact disc that accompanies the book.

In any case, what matters is how the music sounds, how it affects the hearer. It is one of the many miracles of Bach's music that he makes canon and fugue, which every first-year music student must study and write, speak with such eloquence and emotional breadth. All his technical skill would count for nothing if the result was not just technically or intellectually impressive, but profound, moving, and beautiful as well.

But counterpoint is hardly Bach's sole expressive means. Dance rhythms play just as important a role, in obvious ways in the English Suites, French Suites, and Partitas, in which most of the movements are idealized dance forms, each named for the dance they sublimely portray. But many, if not most of the preludes and fugues in *The Well-Tempered Clavier* are set in unmistakable dance rhythm. Some, such as the Fugue No. 2 in C Minor from Book I of *The Well-Tempered Clavier* (CD Tracks 5 and 6) are unmistakable and irresistible. Others, such as the Prelude No. 8 in E-flat minor, employs a sarabande-like beat that impels the music just as strongly, if at a more stately pace. The omnipresence of dance in Bach's music has been recognized more and more, leading to performances that tend toward the quick, alert, and energetic—dance-like—rather than slow and supposedly reverential.

Bach used certain dances again and again, as the middle and last movements of his dance suites. The *sarabande* is the most slow and stately, usually reserved for the composer's deepest meditations. The *allemande* moves at a more flowing pace but is also fairly serious in tone. Moving on to the more moderately paced dances, there are the *minuet*, courtly and often delicate; the *gavotte*; and the *courante,* the last brisk in pace and with more rhythmic bite. Moving up in speed and energy are the *passepied*; the *bourrée*, rough and often fantastical; and finally, the wild *gigue*—the same rhythm as the jig. As one would expect, Bach's versions of these dances are musically distilled essences of the things themselves; but in character they are often surprisingly direct. The composer seems to have sought to hold, perhaps even to amplify the basic emotion that underlies each one And, as we shall see, Bach loved to use other, less common dance forms, too.

Another key element of Bach's music is its mechanical difficulty: it's hard to play. Bach did compose many works for *Klavier*—notably the Two- and Three-Part Inventions and the Anna Magdalena Notebook— as teaching tools, but even the "easy" works in these series are, as noted, well above the beginner's level, and many are quite hard. The Partitas and Toccatas, and the music for organ are the territory of skilled, hard-working performers. Bach himself was one of the great keyboard virtuosos of his day, and refused to compromise. Alongside his brilliant contemporary Domenico Scarlatti, Bach pioneered some virtuoso techniques, most notably hand-crossing. As any student who has played Bach can attest, the challenges of learning a piece, and the attendant sense of triumph at mastering it can be enormous indeed.

But Bach never sacrificed quality for mere technical display. Even his showiest works have a solid base of musical technique, and always say something worth hearing. The very difficult Toccatas always strut their keyboard mastery with the magnificent high spirits and confidence of genius, while the fiery radiance of the virtuosic Partita No. 4 is just the outward aspect of its musical and spiritual profundity.

Bach's curiosity and intellect ranged widely, and he readily digested all things musical. Thus, there are fugues in *The Well-Tempered Clavier* that clearly recall the serene choral polyphony of Giovanni Pierluigi da Palestrina (ca. 1525–1594), or even that of the Flemish Renaissance master Josquin Desprez (ca. 1440–1521). Dances in the suites—the French, English, and the Partitas—are idealized versions of dances with origins from royal courts to taverns. Bach's intellectual curiosity was ambitious and penetrating, and whatever he studied, he studied as deeply and completely as circumstances allowed. We will never know everything musical he investigated, but the major traditions in which he worked are clearly audible in his work. In general, "early" western European music (which is understood to mean anything written up to 1750) needs to divided between sacred music, mostly in solemn polyphony for worship, and secular, which would include dance, songs of love, and early opera.

At Bach's birth and during his lifetime, the dominant musical culture in Europe was Italian. Musical cross-pollination was, however, a powerful force. Heinrich Schütz (1585–1672), who worked in Germany and Denmark studied in Italy, and wrote in an Italian idiom, though the texts he set were mostly in German. Italian composers of church music, such the Roman Palestrina and his peers, wrote their music in a dense style that is descended from that of Flemish composers of the prior two hundred years. All were sophisticated composers of music that can be mind-bogglingly complex, comparable to the works of painters and writers of the time: a "puzzle canon" by the little-known Flemish composer Ghiselin Danckerts (ca. 1510–1565), for example, is annotated on an image of a chessboard, and can be "solved"—that is, played—in twenty different ways.[1] Dufay, Ockeghem, Obrecht, La Rue, Binchois, Busnois, Brumel, Gombert, Isaac, Monte, Rore, Lassus, Tinctoris, and Willaert are all splendid composers whose work seems, sadly, to appeal to an audience doomed to remain small, if fanatical. The masses, motets, and *chansons* of Josquin Desprez, one of the greatest composers in history, is the oldest music likely to move a modern listener. It shows as much technical mastery as Bach's; Josquin relished his own canonic skill as much as Bach would two centuries later, stretching themes out, compressing them, and standing them on their head. So revered was Josquin's mastery that he was compared fifty years after his death to Michelangelo: "For just as no one until now has rivaled Josquin as a composer, so Michelangelo still stands lonely at the summit of all those who have practiced his arts."[2] In Josquin's music are clear anticipations of all polyphony up to and including Bach's.

Opera was not performed in Leipzig, where Bach worked for most of his career—though it was in Dresden, capital of Saxony, the German principality where he lived for most of his adult life and served as court composer. There is disagreement among musical historians as to whether the pious Bach genuinely liked opera or looked down on it as trivial. But the influence of Italian operatic style on Bach's music seems undeniable and tremendous. This effect is, perhaps obviously, more significant in the vocal music—the cantatas, the *St. John* and *St. Matthew* passions and the Mass in B Minor—than in the music for keyboard, and certainly than the organ music, so much of which has its basis in Lutheran hymns. But the passionate, exuberant Italian melodic style is still easy to hear throughout *The Well-Tempered Clavier* and the *Goldberg Variations,* among other works.

Italian influence can be heard most clearly in Bach's concertos (for keyboard as well as other instruments), which he modeled on those of Antonio Vivaldi (1678–1741), whom he admired greatly. Of course, Bach could not resist enriching harmony, while maintaining the broad structural features, sharply profiled melodies, and furious energy of the Italian's style. There are also Bach's spectacular transcriptions of concertos by Vivaldi, Georg Philipp Telemann (a fellow German [1681–1767] who composed in the Italian manner), and others for harpsichord and organ, which are brilliant, absurdly underplayed, and desperately needing revival. Finally, the Italian Concerto for solo keyboard— *Concerto nach italianischem Gusto* ("concerto after the Italian taste") is the composer's amusing title for this—is as spectacular as it is studied in its fulfillment of the style from broad outlines to the smallest detail.

After Italy, France was Europe's most important musical culture, and a glorious one indeed. Clustering around the French royal court, such eminent composers as Jean-Baptiste Lully (born Giovanni Battista Lulli in Florence), Marc-Antoine Charpentier, Jacques de Chambonnières, Louis Couperin and his better-known nephew François, Marin Marais (the composer of wonderful works for viola da gamba), and Bach's great contemporary Jean-Philippe Rameau composed sacred works, as well as opera, ballet, and lighter instrumental pieces in a brightly hued, elegant, melodious style, not lacking in depth and force, either. French music has an elaborate and meticulously codified system of ornamentation, which Bach studied with the closest attention and the most impressive results imaginable. He would come to write out all his ornamentation, leaving nothing to interpreters' questionable taste. On a structural level, all his suites of dance movements (particularly the English Suites and the Partitas—the French Suites ironically least of all) are based on French examples, while carrying the expression they contained to new heights and depths.

French composers wrote many "character" pieces, dances with pretty names in which the music might charmingly imitate bird calls, the buzzing of a fly, or, in one curious example (*L'Anguille* by François Couperin), the writhing of an eel. Although Couperin named all the movements of his wonderful keyboard suites in this way, he was far too good a composer to turn every piece into a musical menagerie; most are abstract dance movements with suggestive titles. (His countryman and heir Claude Debussy would use a similar practice in the first decade of the twentieth century, adding an evocative title at the end of each of his Preludes.) Bach stuck to plain names for the movements of his suites, but one can hear in his dances—the allemandes, sarabandes, courantes, gavottes, and bourrées—the unmistakable energy, rhythm, and sometimes the elegance of the French composers whose work he so admired.

The Germany of Bach's era, while hardly a musical backwater, had except for its church music perhaps the least clearly defined national style. It was, like Italy, a checkerboard of principalities, none large and many quite small. Germany—meaning the German-speaking lands because there was no German nation—had in the seventeenth century endured the Thirty Years' War (1618–1648), which in the name of religion had devastated wide areas, leaving scars that were still evident in the countryside where Bach grew up. And the area was still divided between Lutherans, like Bach himself, and Catholics. Thus, the Lutheran city of Leipzig, where Bach worked for most of his career, was socially conservative. As noted, operas were not performed in Leipzig but staged regularly in Catholic Dresden, the Saxon capital. In spite of religious differences, the residents of central Germany had finally begun to live and work side by side.

Bach's German musical ancestors included Schütz, although that master's influence was probably more on Bach's choral music than his instrumental works. Johann Pachelbel (1653–1706), composer of the famous Canon in D Major heard in countless weddings, movie scores, and television commercials for the last quarter-century, was a friend of Bach's father and undeniably influential on the son. Pachelbel composed a wide variety of choral and instrumental works in forms to which Bach would eventually turn his attention. A very good composer, it would be refreshing to hear more of Pachelbel's oeuvre outside that one inescapable work. The Danish-born north German master Dietrich Buxtehude (1637–1707), whom Bach heard and probably studied with in 1705, is a great composer whose influence on Bach, particularly the works for organ is immense, obvious, and salutary.

Johann Kuhnau (1660–1722) served as Bach's immediate predecessor as cantor—music director—at the Thomaskirche (St. Thomas's Lutheran Church) in Leipzig. He was Bach's most direct German musical ancestor in other ways, as well. Kuhnau published keyboard studies under the title *Clavier-Übung*—clavier practice—which Bach adopted for four volumes of his works for clavier and organ, including, as we shall see, many of the finest. Kuhnau's six *Biblical Sonatas* relate through tone-painting six stories, obviously from the Bible. The first of these, *The Fight Between David and Goliath,* breaks the tale into eight short movements, including Goliath's stamping and ranting, the challenging words exchanged between David and Goliath, and the fight itself, in which the stone is flung into Goliath's forehead, by which he is felled, and even killed, the flight of the Philistines, as well as how the Israelites chase them and slay them by the sword, and finally, the general happiness which shows itself in an abundance of dancing and frolicking.[3] Every bit as charming as it sounds, Kuhnau's piece is a clear, direct influence on Bach's early descriptive keyboard work, the *Capriccio on the Departure of the Beloved Brother,* the six wonderful movements of which depict in music aspects of the event described in the title.

Bach's own compositional style advanced to a point where the edges of national musical footprints were softened. Thus, later works, such as some of the preludes and fugues of Book II of *The Well-Tempered Clavier* or the great Prelude and Fugue in E-flat Major for organ, nicknamed the "St. Anne," echo with rhythms reminiscent of the French overture or alternations in the concerto manner, without being full-on French overtures or concertos. By then Bach had merged national styles, subsuming them to a late, highly polished, supranational style of his own.

It's important to remember, too, that Bach composed more keyboard works than there's room to cover in a relatively brief survey like this, where the big pieces must take precedence. If you look at a CD jacket or an online music vendor, you'll see dozens of preludes, *praeludia*, fugues, and *fughetti* by this musical volcano. Most are short works for his students, but Bach's standards were so high that you won't go wrong by listening to any.

As noted, the German word *Klavier* means "keyboard," a term as vague as it is descriptive, since the clavichord, harpsichord, piano, and organ all have keyboards. The organ works are first to step aside from the confusion, as it is a completely different type of keyboard instrument, and most of what Bach composed for organ was conceived without doubt for that instrument alone.

The tone of the clavichord, silvery and sweet, produced by a simple, hammerlike device called a tangent, is so soft that the music can really only be heard clearly by the performer. Unlike a harpsichordist or pianist, however, the player can alter the tone of a struck note as long as the key remains depressed and the tone itself can be heard. The capability to alter a note makes the clavichord peculiarly expressive. The clavichord's delicate tone makes the instrument impractical for public performance; and recordings generally advise setting the volume low to prevent distortion. The clavichord elicits the adoration of players: "At proper low volume, the instrument can provide a panacea for the cares of the world," wrote the late Igor Kipnis, a fine early music keyboard player.[4] The clavichord was in Bach's time common in middle-class homes, and Bach surely played many and knew the instrument well. Its tiny tone is its most obvious limitation.

Inside the harpsichord, strings are plucked, then damped, by an elaborate mechanism. Unlike the clavichord, the harpsichord has a sounding board to amplify its sound, which would otherwise be just as weak. For greater resonance, some harpsichords have two sets of strings tuned to the same pitch; for even more varied sonority, others have strings tuned an octave above and below that of the tone associated with the struck key, adding an almost orchestral depth and brilliance to the instrument's sound. Others also have a "lute stop," a kind of mute that damps the strings, giving the instrument a more gentle, murmuring quality, reminiscent of the sound of the lute.

Some harpsichords have two keyboards, each with its own set of strings. The player can use both keyboards separately to manage closely written passages or those where a contrasting effect is desired, or coupled, where the rich sonority of both sets of strings is commanded by one of the keyboards. In any case, the tone is the characteristic fluorescent twang familiar to all music lovers; but it offers only one dynamic level—loudness and softness are not variable once the key has been struck. Excellent players find other ways to express what the piano accomplishes with perfect ease. Bach had the harpsichord, often the two-manual kind, in mind when he wrote many of his greatest and most ambitious keyboard works, including the *Goldberg Variations* and the French Overture. A noble instrument capable of genuine grandeur, the harpsichord is far more than a curiosity or a means to achieve a false and precious "old-time" effect. In skilled hands it is inimitably expressive and colorful. Masters to this day, from Falla to Poulenc to Carter, have found it worthy of their attention.

The piano is so well known and loved that there hardly seems reason to explain what it is or how it sounds, but perhaps a few basic facts need to be emphasized. The elaborate, iron-framed contraption has keys that activate hammers, which in turn strike the strings within; the sound produced is then magnified by a soundboard. Two or three foot pedals allow the player to alter the sound in different ways: the *una corda* (one string), or soft pedal on the left moves the keyboard to the side, leaving one string unstruck, thereby reducing the sound produced. The *sostenuto* (sustaining) pedal in the center, not built into all pianos, allows the player to hold certain notes. Most important of the three, the sustaining pedal on the right lifts the dampers so that the keys struck continue to ring afterward. This rightmost pedal sets the piano off from its precursors by allowing players to seem to tie notes together in an effect known as *legato,* allowing the piano to imitate strings, winds, or the human voice. Since the piano is a percussion instrument, its legato is a created effect rather than the real thing. But the sustaining pedal is one of the most important weapons in a pianist's armory, allowing him to produce all sorts of marvelous washes of tone. The piano music of Ravel, Debussy, Liszt, Schumann, Chopin, Schubert, Beethoven, Mozart, and even Haydn are inconceivable without this device. But Bach composed without it, which, as we shall see, has been the source of controversy.

It is also helpful to remember that the original Italian name of the instrument is *pianoforte,* "soft-loud." The name derived from the novelty at the time of its invention of the player's newfound ability to control the volume of tone produced by the force or lack thereof with which he struck the keys. The clavichord produces only the most gentle of tones, whereas the harpsichord's plucked strings sound at one volume, the latter instrument varying its tonal effects in other ways. Piano technology developed further over the nineteenth and twentieth centuries to create today's powerful, flexible instrument, with its roaring bass, brilliant bell-tones, and whiplash ability to thunder, sing, and whisper, even within the confines of one bar of music.

The invention of the instrument, by Bartolomeo Cristofori in Florence in 1700 was, of course, during Bach's lifetime. In 1736 he played instruments built by Gottfried Silbermann. These he found weak but pleasant in tone, though after adjustment he was satisfied with them. Again in 1747 he tried out several in the collection of Frederick the Great.[5] All Bach's contacts with the piano were during its infancy, and he may never have written a note with the piano in mind.

Nevertheless, Bach's works for clavier were played for the nineteenth and early twentieth centuries nearly exclusively on the piano, as musicians and audiences obeyed an evolutionary view that newer, bigger, louder instruments (and ensembles) were necessarily improvements over their eighteenth-century ancestors. A corollary belief was that Bach would have played and composed for newer instruments had he been alive to use them. Probably so: Bach was fascinated by instruments, even collecting and writing for novelties of his day, such as the *lautenwerk,* a lute-harpsichord, and the *geigenwerk,* a curious keyboard hybrid in which strings were brought into contact with wheels, producing a violin-like sound. But not long after 1900, interest in old instruments and curiosity about how Bach's music—and that of other baroque composers—really sounded led to a swelling "original instruments" movement. By 1960, performance on original instruments or reproductions was the dominant trend, and, for ensemble music at least, it remains so today.

The effect of the original instrument movement on keyboard playing, while clear, seems less profound than on other types of performance. Purists might insist on hearing the orchestral parts of the cantatas performed without vibrato on strings, with recorders rather than transverse flutes, or *oboi di caccia* instead of modern oboes, as Bach would have heard his works. Few listeners look these days to symphony orchestras for stylish performances of the Brandenburg Concertos, which are mostly the territory of specialist ensembles and conductors.

But it is only the hardest of the hard-core within the early music movement that denies pianists the right to play Bach. Everyone may understand that he did not write for the instrument in our homes, let alone the nine-foot concert grand of the recital stage; but his music is simply too deeply entrenched in the repertory of student and professional to be dislodged. And in the right hands, it sounds full, clear, and satisfying. What most pianists learn early in their career as Bach players is to use the sustaining pedal—the one on the right that makes notes ring through—rarely, and then with discretion. Its wash of sound is the piano effect most foreign to Bach's music, useful only to bridge the very occasional awkward transition between notes or phrases. In pursuit of clarity in Bach's thematic lines, the Canadian pianist Glenn Gould, whose recordings of the *Goldberg*s and the Partitas are widely admired, developed a light, "fingery," nearly pedal-free technique that suggests the harpsichord. Gould's quest for a piano with the light, responsive action he needed is the stuff of legend as well as the subject of a book, *A Romance on Three Legs: Glenn Gould's Obsessive Quest for the Perfect Piano,* by Katie Hafner. A brilliant contrarian, Gould offends some who admit his skill but find his playing affected and aggressive, with the notes coming at the hearer, as someone described it, "like needles." But for more listeners, Gould's best performances of Bach are not only brilliant in their clarity and vigor, but admirably expressive of the composer's lyrical side as well.

The Arkiv Web site selling classical compact discs offers forty-five versions of Book I of *The Well-Tempered Clavier.* Twenty-nine are on the piano, a respectable twelve for harpsichord, and one—Ralph Kirkpatrick's marvelous recording released in 1963—for the clavichord. The last—Robert Levin's—splits the preludes and fugues equally among harpsichord, clavichord, and organ. This is not to construct a false contest between the instruments, and popularity is rarely a guide to what's right, anyway, but the performances on piano include renowned ones by respected musicians like Gould, Rosalyn Tureck, and Sviatoslav Richter; the last two both employing fully pianistic approaches to the music. Another is by the crossover jazz pianist Keith Jarrett.

On harpsichord, first and foremost, is the incomparable Polish keyboardist Wanda Landowska, who pioneered the instrument in the early twentieth century when it was out of fashion. Landowska's scholarship and breadth of musical knowledge, as well as her virtuosity, uncanny rhythmic drive, passionate expressivity, and deep feeling for what she played make her one of the greatest instrumental musicians ever to be recorded. Landowska's instrument, which she designed herself, is a late-romantic, piano-influenced invention, with extra resonating stops, producing a sonority far larger and richer than the instruments Bach played; readers who demand the authenticity of an original instrument or one built like it must understand that hers will not meet that need. But to pass over Landowska's recordings dogmatically would be a grave error. Anything and everything she did is worth hearing, and of course there are many other fine Bach performances on harpsichord besides hers, as well, including those of Ralph Kirkpatrick, Igor Kipnis, Gustav Leonhardt, and the brilliant French player Pierre Hantaï.

The abstract, linear strength of Bach's music allows it to adapt well to different instruments and interpretive styles. The purity of Bach's lines and his fierce rhythmic drive form a basic material that's nearly indestructible. The shift from harpsichord to piano is far less than, for example, the Swingle Singers' scat vocal arrangements of Bach's music, which can still make enjoyable listening, if perhaps in smaller doses.

It is useful to recall, too, that Bach himself was a tireless transcriber of works from one key to another, and from instrument to instrument; and a rewriter of concertos by Vivaldi, Telemann, Couperin, and others to harpsichord and organ. Ultimately what makes Bach work on any keyboard are the player's passion and ability to render Bach's complex polyphony clearly.

His Life

Johann Sebastian Bach was born on March 21, 1685, in Eisenach, a town in the central German province of Thuringia. His father, Johann Ambrosius, was the town musician of Eisenach, as well as a member of a large family that had already produced musicians in the region for the better part of a century. Bach's mother, Maria Elisabeth, died at age fifty in 1694, when the composer was nine; within a year his father died, also at age fifty. Bach and his older brother Johann Jacob went to live with their eldest brother, Johann Christoph, an organist in the nearby town of Ohrdruf. There, J. S. Bach probably began his life as a journeyman musician under his brother's supervision. He would likely have copied manuscripts, a common practice at the time; it was during this period that the germ of the well-embroidered story of Bach's copying manuscripts by moonlight, forbidden by Johann Christoph, arose.

In 1700, Bach was sent to study at St. Michael's School in Lüneburg, a medium-size city just outside of Hamburg, in northern Germany, a region with a rich tradition of great organ-playing. It seems likely that Bach would have made it his business to hear as many organists as possible, including Georg Böhm in Lüneburg and Johann Reinken in Hamburg. In 1702, Bach graduated from school in Lüneburg and returned to his central German homeland. In August 1703, he was appointed organist at the New Church in Arnstadt. In 1705, Bach turned an authorized leave of one month, to visit the Danish-born organist and composer Dietrich Buxtehude in Lübeck, into a four-month visit. The nature of Bach's relationship with his great predecessor, by then an old man, is undocumented but seems to have been crucial to his artistic development. The visit also got Bach into trouble with his Arnstadt employers, in the first but not the last example of his strong-willed behavior and independent nature.

In 1707, Bach was appointed organist at St. Blasius's church in Mühlhausen, a small Thuringian city, the year he also married a cousin, Maria Barbara Bach. By this time his expertise in the building and reha- bilitation of organs—not to mention his skill as a player—was sufficient for him to get paid as a consultant in such matters. Consulting on organs was to be a major activity and source of income for Bach throughout his life. Although his works are not always easy to date, his development as a composer also advanced during his time in Mühlhausen. Here he began his career as a prolific writer of church and occasional cantatas, which are works to texts for voice and a wide range of accompaniments.

As a young master on the make, Bach received the appointment as court composer to the duke of Weimar, a small German principal- ity. There he moved in 1708, and started his large family. Some of his big organ pieces come from this era, as Bach, evidently excited and inspired, supervised an enlargement of the organ in the duke's chapel. The prince who hired and encouraged Bach died in 1715, and relations with his authoritarian successor were not good, with the composer held in some kind of detention, if not prison, for a month at the end of 1717, then dismissed.

But by then he had secured the position of *Kapellmeister*—music director—for Leopold, the music-loving young prince of Anhalt- Cöthen. This era, from 1718 to 1723, would be one of the most produc- tive in Bach's career. His employer seems not to have placed excessively heavy demands on Bach, allowing him to study and compose at his leisure. It was here that Bach found time to study the music of others, and where he achieved absolute mastery as a composer of instrumental music. Among the masterworks he wrote during the Cöthen years are the Brandenburg Concertos, Book I of *The Well-Tempered Clavier,* the suites for solo cello, and the sonatas and partitas for solo violin.

Bach returned from a trip with the prince in the summer of 1720 to find that his wife had died; within two years he remarried. His second wife, Anna Magdalena Wilcke, a singer of only twenty-one years of age, was of course the same for whom he composed and complied the volume of teaching pieces called the Anna Magdalena Notebook, and possibly the so-called French Suites, too.

Bach's family was large. He fathered twenty children with his two wives, many of whom died in infancy. But three of his sons continued the legacy of musical Bachs. Wilhelm Friedemann, his oldest and apparently favorite son, was one of the most respected organists in Germany and a good composer, though his last years were marked by indigence. Johann Christian Bach, known as "the London Bach" for the city where he settled, was another good composer, whose suave, melodious music is undergoing a well-deserved revival. And greatest is Carl Philipp Emanuel, perhaps the finest master of the early classical era. His brilliant, capricious, passionate music, particularly for keyboard, has enjoyed steady popularity.

Despite Bach's happiness working at Cöthen, he took a bigger job, that of choir director—*Kantor*—at Thomasschule (St. Thomas's School) in the important Saxon city of Leipzig, one of Germany's musical and intellectual capitals. But it entailed heavy and varied responsibilities, from composing church music, to teaching music to students with no interest or talent, to maintaining instruments. As a result, Bach composed some of his greatest works, including cantatas, the two passion settings that have come down to us (*St. John* and *St. Matthew*) and other glories, including the Magnificat, under difficult conditions. Bach also continued to create music outside his job that stand among his grandest achievements, including many of those surveyed here, as well as such mighty creations as the Mass in B Minor, for the king of Saxony, the *Musical Offering* for Frederick the Great of Prussia, and *The Art of Fugue* for his own satisfaction. In this last, one of the great conceptions of abstract music, Bach puts a theme through every contrapuntal process imaginable, but died before he could complete it.

But the Leipzig position, which Bach held until his death in 1750, was far from happy or comfortable. He took the job seriously, but this independent-minded man was not above feuding with colleagues in the school, the churches where his music was performed, and anyone else who crossed him. He also took reprimands and criticism from his bosses—the Leipzig town council—poorly. He could not have been an easy man—the aggressive energy of his music suggests a personality to match—but it's easy to sympathize with Bach, who towered above his nominal superiors in intellect and achievement.

Bach's relationship with the Catholic royal family of Saxony, one of the larger German principalities, and rulers of Leipzig, culminated in the honor of his appointment in1736 as court composer there, but he also held on to the St. Thomas's position and remained in Leipzig. Dresden, the capital of Saxony, had a more liberal, secular musical outlook. Unlike Leipzig, operas were performed and the Italian musical style flourished there. His oldest son, Wilhelm Friedemann, had worked in Dresden since 1733, so Bach already had Saxon ties, and the influence of the lighter, *galant* style of composition in fashion by then can be heard in many of Bach's later works, including Book II of *The Well-Tempered Clavier* and several arias in the Mass in B Minor. He also continued his freelance job of inspecting and reporting on organs throughout central Germany. Much has been made of how limited Bach's horizons were, but a look at a biographical chronology,[1] as in Christoph Wolff's *Johann Sebastian Bach: The Learned Musician,* shows that while Bach did not travel far, he did so regularly at a time when travel was not an everyday activity for most people.

Although Leipzig may not have fully appreciated Bach's stature, his fame in the German states was considerable, at least in musical circles, even in his lifetime. Probably Bach's most famous trip was to Berlin, where, in May 1747, he visited Frederick the Great, the superb flute player and military mastermind of the Prussia's rise. Accompanied by his oldest son Wilhelm Friedemann, he was summoned to the king's presence the moment he arrived in Potsdam, site of the palace. The account of this, as recounted by Johann Nicolaus Forkel, his earliest biographer, is touching. The king was rehearsing for his evening concert:

> With his flute in his hand, he ran over the list, but immediately turned to the assembled musicians and said, with a kind of agitation: "Gentlemen, old Bach is come."[2]

The king canceled his concert for the evening and asked Bach to try out some of the new fortepianos he'd acquired, and Bach improvised a six-part fugue for Frederick and the other musicians. So, clearly Bach's skills remained sharp to the end of his life. On returning to Leipzig, he took the fine theme Frederick had asked him to improvise on and wrote the *Musical Offering,* one of his greatest essays in the old canonic counterpoint, paired with a trio sonata in the fashionable *galant* manner, to display his compositional range.

Bach devoted the last few years of his life to work on the Mass in B Minor and *The Art of Fugue,* that titanic summing-up of the possibilities of the fugal process, which seems to have occupied the composer for the last decade of his life. Interestingly, he did not specify the instrument or instruments on which he wanted it played; it's now heard on keyboards, including the organ, and in arrangement for string quartet or small string orchestras. The Mass, a remarkable blend of old-fashioned counterpoint with operatically conceived arias in a florid, Neapolitan style, is another work on the largest scale and the deepest musical thought.

Bach's eyesight troubled him in the last ten years of his life, possibly the result of diabetes, cataracts, or venereal disease. By 1749, he could hardly see. The following year, Sir John Taylor, a famous British eye surgeon, was summoned to operate, which he did twice that spring. Bach's sturdy system never recovered from the shocks of the crude surgeries; a stroke felled him on July 20, and he died eight days later.

Much of Bach's output consists of church music: there are hundreds of cantatas for weekly and special services, two immense Passion settings that have survived, the big mass setting and four beautiful smaller ones, and many other religious works. Much of his output for the organ consists of setting of hymns called *chorale preludes.* Similar to the visual art from the so-called Middle Ages, Bach's work was created for an occasion, be it a wedding, a funeral, or the big Good Friday service. This is why most of his output is sacred music. Moreover, Bach was a devout Lutheran at a time when everyone was observant: his religious beliefs were literal, sincere, and without irony. His musical treatment of religious themes stays close to the text he is setting, and to the *affect*— the emotion he has chosen to express the words musically. Thus, an aria expressing grief in the *St. John* or the *St. Matthew Passion* will jump, twist, and turn with the sense of the words, and the music will be an unambiguous, richly detailed expression of grief.

Yet of course church music was not the only sort people heard and enjoyed, and Bach had the desire, time, and energy to write in secular forms, too. His religion plays a smaller role in most of the instrumental music we'll examine here, but it's important to remember that religion informed and organized his daily life.

The Toccatas

For Virtuosos Only

L ike *cantata,* meaning "sung," and the opposing term *sonata,* which means "sounded," as in played on an instrument, *toccata,* "touched," is another Italian term that indicated something musically literate Western Europeans of the sixteenth through eighteenth centuries understood at once. *Toccata* is a more specific word than the others, however, generally meaning a brilliant keyboard piece designed to show off a player's skill—his "touch." The ever-daring Claudio Monteverdi used the title for the short but powerful instrumental prelude to his opera *L'Orfeo,* so it was not only and absolutely for keyboard showpieces, but that's the most common use of the name. The best known toccatas before Bach's are probably those by Girolamo Frescobaldi (1583–1643), one of the first important composers to focus on keyboard music. Frescobaldi's toccatas follow a defined pattern, opening with brooding scale work before moving on to more articulate and impassioned outbursts, then falling gradually to a quiet close, more or less in the mood of the opening. Their structures tend to be simpler than Bach's, and they lack the big fugal sections Bach inserted; although they need a skilled player to do them justice, they are not as showy as those we're about to look at. But these are fine works of a lyrical cast that hold up well today.

Bach's seven keyboard toccatas form a category within the composer's work, distinct from other pieces with similar titles such as "toccata and fugue." They are interesting because we hear in them another side of Bach the musician. Technically they are among his most demanding works, written by a virtuoso for virtuosos.

The simplest way to look at the structure of Bach's toccatas is to note that they open with bravura passagework, which is followed by a slow section, meditative in tone, and conclude with a lively and generously proportioned fugue. But this is perhaps to oversimplify, as Bach found many occasions to speed up and slow down dramatically, and to engage in other types of musical rhetoric. The toccatas are meant to sound like improvisations, and each may have begun that way, but by the time Bach wrote them down, every effect was calculated: the toccatas are a kind of musical playacting, masques comprised of grand, exciting gestures. That said, too, one would be hard pressed to place them among his very finest works, enjoyable though they are. Some seem to have been composed early in his career, and lack the structural tightness he would master by 1720; the fugues in several are simple and run on longer than necessary. The two held in highest regard are the F-sharp minor and the C minor, both apparently dating from around 1720, by which time Bach had achieved full maturity as a composer.

The Toccata in F-sharp minor opens with a long and complex sequence, beginning with a huge flourish, full of grandeur and drama. A passage with the tempo marking *adagio,* and resembling a sarabande, follows. As we shall see, this slow, thoughtful dance form is the center of gravity in the French and English Suites and the Partitas. The mood is remote, icy, brooding, a profound meditation at the heart of all the Toccata's busyness. It leads quietly into the long three-voice fugue, based on a fiery falling subject. This finger-twisting section Bach marks *presto e staccato*—fast and in detached notes.

Rather than end it in a conventional way, Bach makes the transition to the next section unusual in that he pulls the fugue apart, in a bold transition to the fourth section, a striking sequence in a quasi-improvisatory style. Here, the music hovers in a territory of indecisive, shifting harmony, pitching in a few tonal directions before settling on one. As every commentator is duty-bound to point out, this section probably gives a sense of Bach's own skill as an improviser, as well as his ability to slip effortlessly from one key to another; it does sound as though he's vamping, if on a high imaginative plane. But finally the last big section begins with the decisive appearance the subject of a second, three-part fugue, based on a sliding subject in a graceful 6/8 beat. Bach works in freer counterpoint as the fugue progresses. This eminently satisfying work ends on a flourish that recalls the opening and an apotheosis of the subject of the second fugue.

The C minor Toccata is probably the most popular and perhaps the finest of the series. It's a superb, tightly organized work that's exciting to hear from start to finish. It's also another example of Bach, like other composers in the baroque era, writing music in a minor key that simply cannot be perceived as sad. Sometimes pensive, at others forceful, and downright playful in the fugue, this shows Bach in his cheerful C minor mood, shared with the Partita No. 2 and the great, dancing fugue in the same key in Book I of *The Well-Tempered Clavier.*

The work opens with a series of eloquent runs in a firm rhythmic profile that's hard to forget. This very polished passage has a rhetorical quality, as though the composer is signing his name musically, underlined with a proud flourish. The second section consists of an intensely meditative passage founded on a long, incisive melody. Bach enriches this with complications of harmony and rhythm, but never in all his lush embroideries loses the thematic thread. The three-voice fugue is based on a rocking subject that's undeniably jolly, almost like a sailor's dance. Of course, Bach's treatment is as challenging intellectually as it could be in the context of a showpiece like this, but the powerful rhythm of the subject drives everything ahead forcefully. Suddenly the fugue dissolves into a big flourish and a few, dramatic notes in slow tempo; then recommences. But this time, it's as a double fugue, meaning Bach weaves in another subject. Indeed the texture is unmistakably richer, but he lightens the already cheerful tone with some playful rhythmic ornamentation. The C minor Toccata, fantastical, brilliant, and irresistible, ends on a sequence of rapid passagework, in alternating slow and quick tempos.

The D major Toccata seems to be of a vintage about a decade earlier than the two we've looked at, and musically it may be less substantial. But this exhilarating virtuoso romp is remarkably effective and fun in the right hands, as three recorded performances made in the course of sixty years, each radically different from the others, show. Wanda Landowska's, from 1936 and made on her massive, sonorous custom harpsichord, is typical of her work, filled with her own immense personality and staggering in its dash and dancelike, earthy vibrancy. Glenn Gould's, recorded in the early 1960s on his doctored, equally inauthentic piano, is more moody and affected, like the man himself, but as thrilling in its individuality as Landowska's rendition; his darker view of the middle section sets off the blazing final part quite effectively. And a 1997 recording by the brilliant French harpsichordist Pierre Hantaï on a modern reproduction of an instrument from Bach's time, offers all the stylistic acuity and splendor that a skilled early music specialist of this era can achieve. It's no less fine than those by his famous predecessors, and one would be silly to call one better than the others. Listen to all three; this wonderfully conceived work sounds remarkably good in the hands of all three players.

Cast in four broad sections, the Toccata opens with a big flourish reminiscent of Bach's works of the same title for organ. It's marked by phrases in tremolando, a kind of trembling figure. This impressive opening is followed by a cheerful section in a brisk tempo, and marked by a strong rhythmic impetus. The third and longest section, itself cast in three splendidly interwoven passages, opens in a slow tempo (adagio), and features an eloquent, speech-like falling figure, interspersed by tremolandi, all acting as introduction to a long, sorrowful fugal passage in F-sharp minor based on a winding subject. Bach brings back the material of the slow introduction at the end of the fugue to make the link with and transition to the final part, a driving fast fugue based on a quick-time dance subject. The affect of this rollicking final section contrasts as powerfully as it might with the gravity of what it follows; the wild closing phrases, in blazing double-time passagework bring the Toccata to an ending that's a roller coaster of virtuosic keyboard thrills.

The D minor Toccata is another relatively early work, thought to date to about 1710. It's also an uneven piece containing two long fugues that shows how far Bach would travel in his ability to condense his counterpoint to make it speak to the mind and heart. But its three other sections are very interesting. The opening part, complex and beautiful, starts with a sensitive, twisting figuration, followed by powerful chords and runs. The music then moves to a lyrical meditation in which one can easily hear the composer's influence on Schumann, whose early piano music is filed with moments like this, in which a songlike theme is repeated a number of times, with subtle shifts of harmony. The third part of the Toccata is a long fugue on an aggressive, rising subject in a powerful dance rhythm. Insufficiently varied and overlong, the young Bach's inexperience in pacing fugal material at this early point in his career is obvious.

The composer finally pulls the fugue apart dramatically into strands, then beginning a hovering adagio passage that speaks clearly of his skill as an improviser. This skillful sequence anticipates the fourth section of the F-sharp minor Toccata of a decade later, as well, once again, of Schumann, whose early piano masterworks contain many moments of similar lyrical introspection that show his deep knowledge of and immense debt to Bach. Toward the end of the passage, Bach tugs at his harmonic fabric ever more bravely. The last part is another fugue in a choreographic mode that's cheerful but long and less than fascinating.

The Toccata in E minor is another work dated to about 1710. Slightly shorter and more consistent in tone than the D minor work, its moody affects and more delicate keyboard textures form a convincing whole; this is a fine piece that could bear more frequent hearing and performance. The E minor Toccata opens with a compound introduction. An intense, twisting figure in the lower notes marked by almost constant syncopations kicks things off in a mood of nervous intensity. A four-voice contrapuntal passage marked by Bach *un poco allegro*—somewhat quickly—follows. This is also intense and serious, if more steady rhythmically than the opening passage, making the structure of this work similar to that of the D major Toccata, where a steady passage follows a flighty, fantastical one. And the third section, a wild quasi-improvisation featuring scales, curling figuration, and agitated tremolandi in a slow tempo, also follows the same pattern. This section ends with a passionate and beautiful passage in a panting rhythm.

The last section of the Toccata is a three-voice fugue in a nervous, melancholy affect and graceful keyboard figuration the E minor tonality often inspires in the composer, quite similar in sound and texture to the prelude and fugue in E minor of Book I of *The Well-Tempered Clavier*. This fugue opens with a sensitive, flowing subject that dominates the texture, which Bach keeps light, even when all three voices are in play. Some faster notes just before the very end increase the sense of agitation. The mood and tone of this essay seem melancholy rather than tragic, and the rushing figuration carries the willing listener along easily in its sad but lovely tide.

The G minor is one of the simplest and may be the least successful of the keyboard toccatas. Two of its five sections are long fugues that are repetitious and lacking in rhythmic variety. But it does open with a fine descending flourish that sweeps directly into a brooding adagio section of notable gravity and force. The first fugue, in four parts on a cheerful and bouncy subject in B-flat major, follows. But again, Bach seems here not to have mastered the rhythmic and textural variety that gives his later fugal writing such strength and interest. The fugue dissolves into another brooding slow passage, reminiscent of the earlier one, which acts as introduction to the second fugue, an even longer and more monotonous exercise in the skipping rhythm of a gigue, which can and should enliven but here seems deadening, as the composer stays too long in the same pattern. Good players can make a case for it, though; and Bach would go on to write many a fine fugue in the same rhythm. The work ends forcefully on a recollection of the opening passagework.

The G major Toccata seems to be the earliest of these works. Cast in three big sections, it has a strong Italian style and much in common with the concerto form. One can hear in the fantastic rhythmic drive and virtuoso writing of the glittering opening movement an anticipation of Bach's great Italian Concerto (CD Tracks 10 through 12) of twenty-five years later. The keyboard writing is demanding, alternating falling chords with rattling scales and passagework, and the affect displays a pure, virile joy and excitement. A thoughtful slow movement, also in the lyrical Italian manner, holds the center of the work; while a bit simple compared to some of Bach's other passages in this style, it's nevertheless a touching and effective moment of rest. The third section is a three-part fugue on a joyful subject in the skipping rhythm of a dance called the *siciliano*. Here, too, it may be that Bach loses his way, as the fugue seems to wander on for longer than necessary. But even with its flaws, this work offers much in the way of youthful energy and charm.

The Inventions
and Sinfonias
Sophisticated Teaching Tools

Bach composed the Inventions, also called the Two-Part Inventions, and the Sinfonias, referred to as the Three-Part Inventions, as early steps in his keyboard teaching method. Though brief, Bach did not compromise content or craftsmanship, making of each a little gem: "Only a gentle gravity betrays their didactic intention,"[1] as Charles Rosen observes. The references in the titles to two and three parts defines the number of polyphonic lines in the work: in the Inventions, except for closing chords, each hand is called upon to play one note at a time; in the Sinfonias, a total of three notes, a considerable increase in the difficulty of execution, as anyone who has studied them can attest.

Although obviously light in texture, the two- and three-part Inventions are remarkably satisfying because of their musical integrity—you don't feel deprived, wishing for more lines, because the ones Bach writes are so rich. They also display an architectural perfection that stems from their brevity: none is more than two pages in score, the longest—the E major Invention—at sixty-two measures, taking about three minutes to play. The sublime fifth and ninth Sinfonias, both in slow tempos, run about three and one-half minutes. Bach masterfully balances the technical challenge he is posing, different in each work, with an artful presentation, tailoring his material for the short format. These brief works were immensely influential on such composers as Chopin, Liszt, and Debussy, whose respect for short forms was deep and skill in using them formidable.

The first invention, in the plain key of C major, will be familiar to many piano students. It looks fairly simple on paper: some scales, a few little turns, mostly two notes in one hand against one in the other, except for a short passage in bars 13 and 14. Of course, it's much more difficult to execute well than its apparent simplicity suggests. In some passages, Bach has the player work in a tight hand position, whereas in others the performer must reach; the little turns are hard to place correctly against their accompanying notes in the left hand. And the open texture makes every smudged note and rhythmic falter stand out painfully.

The main theme is built on the C major scale, perhaps the plainest statement in a composer's thematic vocabulary. Bach passes the sliding theme from hand to hand, inverts it, then moves to G major, embarking on a beautiful, shimmering passage that hints at a rainbow of other keys. The two hands pass the theme back and forth in a passage that is probably the easiest in the work, reaching toward a climactic high C, and on to a conclusion that's tranquil and almost triumphant. Bach also wrote a second version of the Invention in triplets, a common rhythmic device that squeezes three notes into the space of two, creating a pulsing or throbbing feel. In this little work the triplets give it a more decorated, notey surface. It's lovely, too, and harder to play than the plain version.

The C minor Invention is an intense little movement that feels like an allemande, the graceful but serious dance that is the opening movement of most of the French Suites, and second movement in the English Suites and Partitas. Musically Bach pursues canonic writing, a strict form of counterpoint that always sounds free and passionately expressive in his hands, as it does here. As in the first Invention, the two lines twist together, and reach up and down, as Bach inverts his moody theme. He ends the work severely, on two bare Cs, the two voices of his canon and the two parts of his Invention.

The third Invention, in D major, is in the light-footed rhythm of a passepied, another old dance Bach uses often in the suites. The piece opens with a sweet-natured tune in the right hand, which the left soon joins, adding the hopping accompaniment characteristic of the passepied. Later in the work, Bach moves the jumping figure to the right hand. This gentle music has a pastoral feel, and, obviously, a light texture. But as in the C major invention, little trills and turns—and here there are many—challenge the player's skill at clean execution. As with most of these two-part pieces, the exposed lines leave little room for error.

The D minor Invention is the dark sibling of the one that precedes it. This moment of tightly woven demonic choreography is colored by the expressively dissonant interval of the diminished seventh. Its slithering opening theme states that interval in the steep fall immediately, after which the right hand moves to a sequence of three rising longer notes as the left hand takes up the opening theme. A rising figure moves to the left hand in a long sequence of great energy and élan. This concludes as the hands move together in a passage of twisting fast notes that lead the first section to a clear finish. The middle part begins with the three-note figure, rendered as a hop in the right hand. This breaks into a long trill above steady, furious activity in the left, into which Bach weaves a twisting figure. He then turns the material around, giving the trill to the left hand, and the busy part to the right, where harmonic activity also intensifies when the left hand bursts into activity again. This soon leads to the climax of the second portion in an exciting passage, and the restatement of the opening. Bach inverts the three-note figure into a forceful restatement at, leading into a finger-twisting passage, then the dark conclusion of this minute of astonishing music, packed densely with interesting and exciting ideas.

If you listen to the Inventions on your CD player, it's worth playing the opening phrases of the D major, then the D minor, to hear how similar they are in structure, though their affects—their moods—are in dramatic, even violent, opposition. It's thought that Bach conceived the Inventions and Sinfonias in complementary pairs. He built the first four Inventions on the scale pattern, the plain, steplike motions of which are what novice keyboard players typically study.

With the fifth Invention, in E-flat major, Bach changes his pattern. Both voices enter at the same time, instead of higher first, as before. This is a good-humored piece, where he puts his bumpy theme through some twilit harmonic alterations in the middle before bringing it home to the home key. As with the first three, the score contains turns and trills that require careful coordination of the hands.

The E major Invention, one of the biggest in this group, opens with a dancelike theme in a syncopated rhythmic format, which means that the emphasis is on a weak beat. But the profile soon comes into clearer focus as a sequence of excited, faster moving notes move against a steadier background, then Bach puts this jumpy figure into both hands, to great effect. But again and again he pulls the rhythm apart, which has a curious result of highlighting his harmonic excursions. This is the only of the Inventions of Sinfonias conceived in two sections, both of which are to be repeated; this accounts for its unusual length. Its allemande-like companion work in E minor opens with a sad, drooping theme, marked by some elegant trills and turns in the right hand over a more decisive falling interval in the left. The hands pass these around, with long trills in both punctuating the melancholy discussion.

Bursting with high spirits and buoyant, dancing rhythms, the F major Invention (CD Track 1) presents a shocking contrast with the introverted E minor work it follows; it's also well known and loved for its radiant joy.

The F major Invention consists of three closely related thematic ideas: the bouncing figure heard at the beginning (passing to the left hand almost immediately at 0:03), a falling pattern in the right (also at 0:03), and a note pattern in even, fast notes in both hands, first heard at 0:08 that seems to yelp for joy. When listening, remember that these three ideas are so closely tied that the second springs from the first and the third spouts naturally from the second. It's also a pity to pick apart this jolly peasant dance, brilliantly assembled though it is. Do, however, note the enriched harmonic scheme at its center, starting at 0:26, and the return to yodeling at 0:48. Good players can dispatch this with what sounds like ease, but its leaps and fast passagework can be a cruel challenge.

The graceful F minor Invention is built on an arching theme that is reminiscent of the C-sharp minor prelude of Book I of *The Well-Tempered Clavier,* though it's shorter and of course much lighter in texture. Nevertheless, here both hands are busy throughout, as Bach weaves his parts into a dense-sounding web of considerable richness, at least in the context of two lines of polyphony. The right hand reaches upward regularly for expressive high notes, and the left has some big jumps to deal with, as well. A sequence of trills marks the center point, then the conclusion, of this exquisite and somber gem.

The G major Invention that follows is a study in a lilting beat (9/8) Bach liked and used often when representing joy. The right hand opens with the burbling theme, rife with turns and trills. Apparently one of the composer's main goals here was to teach the rendering of trills correctly, which is nowhere near as easy as it may appear: they are never merely a blur of fast notes in one hand; rather, a sequence of notes, led into, calculated, then exited, always placed against the activity of the other hand. In any case, the G major Invention is a deeply joyful dance in a pastoral mood. Its companion in G minor opens ominously with a G in the bass, followed by a rising melodic figure in the right hand, which is, however, heavily weighted with chromatic accents. Again, two-against-one patterns and turns dominate the melodic texture, and the rhythm is light and quick, but the mood seems curiously doom-laden for so slender a work.

Extending the broad rhythmic structure of the G major Invention yet further, Bach stretches out to 12/8—a long, loping beat—for the A major Invention. Here the hands trade off a racing figure and a beautiful, dancelike theme based on repeated notes and the inevitable turns and trills. This is another piece that is filled with joy, if not precisely merry in the manner of the F major Invention (CD Track 1). But about two-thirds of the way through, Bach calls on his students over the ages to use both hands to disentangle some finger-twisting patterns. The A minor Invention sounds very much like a movement from the Partita No. 3, in the same key. As in that unusual work, the hands here must trade some cascading figuration with a dancelike sparkle.

The B-flat major Invention is a study of turns, which both hands exchange, then share. A hopping figure reminiscent of that in the F major Invention moves things along rhythmically, also keeping the mood light. Yet for all its good humor, the little piece radiates an almost beatific delight. The final Two-Part Invention in B minor presents an eccentric charm. It opens with a mincing melody in the right hand above a steady beat struck by the left; there are, once again, many trills that require careful placement. Bach extends the quick-note tail of the main theme into a rumbling sequence in the bass, faintly comedic in effect. But the affect of this little work is curiously inscrutable.

The Sinfonias are technical studies in three voices that will inevitably remind the listener of their companion works. They are no longer than the Two-Part Inventions. But what a difference that third polyphonic strand makes in the sound: these are far richer and more complex. And they are, of course, more challenging. As we will see, only one, No. 5 in E-flat major is playable by beginners, and that only in the simplest of several versions.

The difference is audible a few seconds into the C major Sinfonia, first of the series. As in the C major Invention, Bach opens with a rising scale, but the sound is rich and open. When the third voice enters, the richness of sound almost overwhelms, if heard directly after the austere textures of the Inventions. The two C major works may remind some of the preludes in the same key that open Books I and II of *The Well-Tempered Clavier,* the first having a prefatory feel, and contained in texture and range; the second with a more Jovian breadth and motion.

The C minor Sinfonia that follows is a complex and profoundly beautiful work. This lilting dance, set in the 12/8 beat of which Bach was so fond, sets a swaying theme against a rocking one, then later a running figure, providing rhythmic contrast. The challenge for a player to manage these three thematic incarnations, all in the 12/8 beat, is considerable. The work presents a melancholy affect that is, however, ineffably sweet as well. Listeners who know Bach's *St. Matthew Passion* may recognize in this two-page study a kinship with "Erbarme dich" ("Have mercy"), the great, large-scale aria of contrition in Part II of that immense sacred drama.

The third Sinfonia, in D major, has some of the feeling of an allemande, albeit at a quicker tempo and breezier mood than most of the inward-looking dances of that name by Bach. This opens with a perky phrase that eventually winds into longer sequences, though the opening phrase and its songful good cheer never disappear. The D minor Sinfonia is a sad and languid affair, unlike the energetic two-part Invention in the same key. It opens with a sighing phrase in the right hand above slower patterns in the left; the sighing melody soon joins as the middle voice. These intertwine over the course of the movement, but for once Bach tends to hold the slower-moving notes to the left hand, almost in the manner of an accompaniment; he never really inverts the thematic material, as he often likes to do. Thus the Sinfonia has a chamber music feel, as though we are hearing three separate instruments. Bach brings it to a leisurely end in a long, lovely, drooping phrase.

The beautiful Sinfonia No. 5, in E-flat major, comes in two versions, the first plain and relatively playable by a beginner, and an ornamented one, which is hard. Professionals always play the ornamented one (because they can), so the plain version, which is still wonderful, is rarely heard outside the practice room or teacher's studio. In any case, this celestial colloquy for three voices shows Bach in the sublime mood E-flat major often puts him in. As in the previous Sinfonia, the left hand maintains an accompaniment that's articulate, even eloquent, but also steady. Based on arpeggiated chords, it's inherently different from the two upper voices, which engage in a sweetly melodious dialogue based on what are known as *suspensions.* These are the resolution of dissonances in a way that makes them sound as though they are melting back into consonance. From a technical standpoint, this Sinfonia is a study in holding down some notes while releasing others, and a test of the player's delicacy of tone and touch. The character of the music demands a very moderate pace, and dynamics (volume) barely above a murmur; the mood Bach creates is rapturous and magical.

Open keyboard textures and a broad rhythmic frame give the E major Sinfonia an improvisatory feeling. This almost seems a more relaxed take on the rhythmic patterns worked out in tighter form in the C minor Sinfonia, as a dancing figure skips ahead of steadier notes first heard in the bass. The third voice, with the longest notes of all, enters last. The voices playfully change parts, and there is a climactic moment where the music pauses rather grandly for breath before scampering into the final bars. The E minor Sinfonia is a serious piece, marked by a long, sad melody in the right hand, entering over a cellolike figure that echoes it in the bass; the third voice, too, echoes this primary melodic strand. Finally, one voice or another carries a steady stream of faster-flowing notes all the way to the end, as the melody twines though the other two parts. The mood is deeply melancholy but not tragic. It's easy to hear how a work like this influenced Chopin's idea of keyboard writing and sound, with its three voices flowing separately but clearly, in a single, impassioned stream.

The F major Sinfonia bounces along, animated by one of Bach's favorite rhythmic figures for the expression of joy (short-short-long-long). Its patterns are not unlike the F major Invention (CD Track 1), if in a more contained package than that soaring work's jubilation. This marvelous study is urbane in character, where the F major Invention is wild.

The great Sinfonia No. 9 in F minor (CD Track 2) is perhaps the high point of the set. Bach packs into its thirty-five measures as much passionate expressivity as seems possible by his intensive use of chromatic harmony. This means he uses the intervals in between the normal full steps to give the music a sighing, almost shattered sound, and a grief-laden affect that remind more than a few listeners of the composer's two surviving Passions. Certainly this jewel-like work shares its unusual expressive language with some of the reflective arias from the *St. John* and *St. Matthew* passions; it's also close in spirit and harmonic construction to the twenty-fifth of the *Goldberg Variations,* where Bach subjects the melody to the same kind of powerful chromatic distortion, making it sound also like a long, vast sigh.

The bass line opens the piece, above which the sighing theme—the second of the three parts—immediately appears. The third voice, repeating the second, appears in the highest pitch at 0:15. Note right after the first note how the bass jumps up, then begins a long slow descent, ending at 0:14. This kind of line, called a *lamento bass,* was used by composers before and through the baroque era to express grief. Listen then to the powerful version of the opening sigh motif taken up by the left hand (0:16). Other landmarks worth listening for are the passage from 0:28 to 0:41, where the bass line drops out, giving the twining upper voices their say; and the closed phrase at 1:16, after which the voices resume in major key. This gives a hint of consolation to the next section. Yet this, too, is drenched in musical sighs, and before long the major key evaporates. But, in fact, the main thematic elements remain close to center stage throughout.

Perhaps it's most useful when listening to this astonishing work to notice how Bach persistently pulls the thematic strands away from the direction we expect the melodies to go. Examples of this melodic gravity can be heard in rising phrases that fail to hit their marks at 0:58, 1:01, 2:04, 2:13, 2:37, and in the glorious falling phrase at 3:17. And only rarely does the composer allow the dissonance-spiked harmony to resolve. Clearly, his affective goal here is not the expression of joy.

These two pages, revered by those who know them, stand as one of Bach's most penetrating expressions of sorrow.

The G major Sinfonia is an elegant follow-up to the little masterwork that went before. Here the lines move in patterns that are almost regular for Bach, one of music's great lovers of irregularity. The motion of this suave movement is dominated by sixteenth notes, the quickest of those presented. Infinitely graceful, the G minor Sinfonia is a glorious movement with a profound dance feel. Yet it seems more a choreographic poem than an actual passepied, which it most resembles. Listeners familiar with the late piano works of Brahms will surely recognize an ancestor in its gentle melancholy and sweeping keyboard textures.

Bach must have conceived the A major Sinfonia in the style of a trio sonata for flute. From the opening, the trembling top line has the unmistakably feel of a wind instrument. Bach mixes and moves the three voices around thoroughly, in the style of a chamber sonata, before the polished musical rhetoric of the final phrases. The beautiful A minor Sinfonia is, like the G minor, an idealized dance of grace and profundity that casts long shadows over the keyboard music that followed. This one also starts in a short, mincing rhythm rather like a passepied, but then broadens splendidly into a more waltzlike motion, and later even achieves a barcarolle-like sweep. All this is over the space of sixty-four easy-flowing measures.

The B-flat major Sinfonia is another urbane essay in trio sonata style in which Bach passes the thematic strands from voice to voice with supreme ease and good humor. He engages in some rhythmic compression toward the end that keeps listeners from getting too comfortable. An amiable scramble brings this relaxed sounding but very complex piece to an end.

The fifteenth and last Sinfonia, in B minor, is a fantastical piece in a throbbing dance beat. One voice carries an urgent sounding theme; another, a fretful accompaniment. Then one rests while the other opens a glorious peacock's tail of shuddering figuration. These are tossed around, and a third voice enters, enriching the texture and harmony. The composer ties them all together in a dramatic pause, repeats the flourish and the jumpy dance theme to end it decisively. It's a great conclusion to these extraordinary miniatures.

Dance Suites I
The English and the French

One cliché about Bach's keyboard music states that the English Suites are more French in style than are the French Suites, and that the Partitas (once confusingly nicknamed the "German Suites") are more French than either; another states that there is nothing in any way "English" about the English Suites. Not all the experts agree: in his study *J. S. Bach: A Life in Music,* Peter Williams writes, "The English Suites are the most French of Bach's sets, especially as copied and ornamented by his pupil H. N. Gerber."[1] Williams's distinction seems correct; but be that as it may, these observations may help a listener seeking to understand the history and styles of both groups of suites. In all cases, Bach based these marvelous works on French models for the individual dances that make them up, the ordering of the movements, and their elaborately conceived ornamentation; unmistakable Italian influence may also be heard in others, notably in the concerto-like passages of the opening movements of several English Suites. Bach's own brand of melodic and harmonic intensity give these works a sound and gravity quite distinct from anything he is likely to have used as an example.

These fusses over the names, then over which set is "more French" than the other, are amusing when set against the fact that Bach himself named neither group of suites. The French Suites had their origin in the Anna Magdalena Notebook in 1722, were polished by the composer over the next couple of years, and were modestly titled in French *Suites pour le Clavessin*—"Suites for the Keyboard."[2] But how and when the nickname got attached is not known. Almost nothing is understood of how the English Suites were named, apart from a story, never substantiated, which sprang from a phrase of Bach's son Johann Christoph, that they were "*fait pour les Anglois.*" Bach composed the larger, more ambitious English Suites first. Their date of composition is uncertain, but recent scholarship places them near the end of his time in Weimar, which he left in 1717.[3] The French Suites—shorter and less technically demanding—date from the composer's time in Cöthen. His second wife, Anna Magdalena, copied some of them in her own hand, and it is thought that Bach may have composed them as keyboard teaching tools for her. Although these are lighter in texture and generally easier to play, they are every bit as fine as the earlier English Suites.

The relative Frenchness of the two sets of suites matters only because both are structured like dance suites by French composers (and some Germans such as Froberger and Buxtehude, who sometimes wrote in the French style), and because their ornamentation, far more elaborate in the English Suites, also reflect Bach's careful study of French musical models. *Ornamentation* means simply the flurries of little notes that decorate the main tones; the two are easy to tell apart when listening. Bach absorbed one source, six suites by French composer Charles Dieupart (ca. 1667–1740), while copying them for his own use. Bach's own notebook containing Dieupart's suites is in a Frankfurt university library.

The sets of suites resemble each other structurally, made up of consistent patterns of short, incisive dance movements. The big difference is that all the English Suites open with a Prélude—Bach's own term—of considerable dimensions. Also, in all the English Suites, the second movement is an allemande, in moderate tempo, and the final movement a gigue, in a quick tempo and skipping rhythm. In between come a courante, and a slow sarabande, profound, exalted, sometimes tragic in feeling. What varies from suite to suite are the *galanteries*, the light, often elegant dance movements interspersed through the middle. These airs, *loures,* minuets, bourrées, gavottes, anglaises, polonaises, and passepieds are all optional, but as we shall hear, add great charm and piquancy.

Bach appears to have given some thought to the publication sequence of the six works in each set. The English Suites begin with the lightest and shortest work, with each succeeding suite being longer, weightier, and more imposing. The last of them, in D minor, opens with a prelude of huge dimensions that runs several minutes longer than any of its fellows. In the subtle French Suites, this tendency seems slightly less pronounced, though the last three of these are certainly larger in scope than the first three, Bach adding more *galanterie* movements to the French Suites as they progress. The first Suite has only five movements overall; the second and third, six; the fourth and fifth, seven; and the sixth—undoubtedly the largest of the group—eight movements. Bach later found interesting ways of varying these patterns for the Partitas.

Baroque ornaments are codified in a series of bewildering symbols in a musical score, with which the English Suites in particular abound; their purpose is to add a passionate, almost operatic elaboration to the melodic lines. Bach compiled a little summary of them, often reproduced, for his eldest son, Wilhelm Friedemann. There are many kinds of ornaments, but even the master's diagram was incomplete. Each symbol bears a name and a theoretically exact manner of rendering, all of which in practice are far from solid. Ornamentation is a complex technical matter for the professional, beyond the scope of this survey. In his performance guide to the English Suites the British-born Canadian harpsichordist Colin Tilney observes with a performer's hard-won wisdom that "Bach's ornamentation asks for intelligent co-operation, not unthinking subservience. . . ."[4] But surely the listener who attends closely to the little notes that scoop into and away from the main tones will be better for his or her efforts.

Published editions of the English Suites are based on a copy made by Bach's pupil Heinrich Nikolaus Gerber in the 1720s, Bach's own manuscript not having been found. Thus, we may assume that Gerber added ornamentation as he was taught, or as he heard the composer play and teach the music. As noted, the lighter textures and easier writing of the French Suites make it clear that the composer used them as teaching tools; moreover:

> The many copies by Bach's pupils that have survived show what importance was attached to these Suites not only in the house music of the Bach family but also in Bach's teaching, as a bridge between the Inventions and the Well-tempered Clavier.[5]

Bach the working musician often wrote with more than one purpose. Inspiration may have been unfailing, but it was not necessarily
high on his own list of reasons to compose.

The Prélude of the first English Suite, in A major, opens the series
with a handsome flourish up the keyboard, followed a lilting movement
in an easy rhythm. Although shorter and lighter in mood than any of the
others, it sets the form of the opening sections, being improvisational
in tone, composed freely from start to finish, without repeats or a strict
development. The thoughtful allemande that follows is, however, large
in scale and more disciplined in form, consisting like all allemandes of
two halves, the second of which mirrors and replies to the first, in this
resembling most of the other two-part dances by Bach. He also traverses
several keys before returning home in the closing phrases. Typically,
too, the second halves of these movements present more complex
counterpoint and harmony than the first. This particular allemande
is, in any case, distinguished by its lovely, interweaving lines. The
courante that comes next presents a more gentle side of this frequently
aggressive dance. A second courante, complementary in melody and
character, follows, *"avec deux Doubles,"* as the score reads. A *double* is
simply a variation. The first of these, over a jogging bass line is lavishly
ornamented; the second moves freely as energetic rhythmic figures
pass from hand to hand. In some performances the order of these two
variations is reversed.

The sarabande, sublime in mood and expression, will remind many
of that on which the *Goldberg Variations* are based. Two cheerful bourrées follow, the first with a mock-rustic note that anticipates some of
Chopin's mazurkas, the second a muttering page in the minor key,
provides contrast in tone color and mood. As is typical with these
movements, the first dance is played again, but without repeats. The
concluding gigue, based on a trill-laden theme and driven by a fantastic
rhythmic animation, provides a rollicking conclusion to the work. It's
also notable for having two dynamic indications, where the composer
marks passages that he wants to be played softly. These are relatively
rare in baroque music, where the character of any piece, as indicated
by the title, dictated its volume, and its speed, as well.

The fine bones of the French Suites as a group are evident from the first notes of the delicate and melancholy allemande that opens the first Suite, in D minor. All six open with allemandes, moderate in tempo, setting the more inward tone that marks these works as a group. The courante, sharper in rhythm, is a fine example of the serious posture, even the intensity, this dance often displays in Bach's hands. The brief sarabande that follows is relatively easy to play, but its reflective melody and the deeply expressive dissonances that support the tune carry the movement to a high artistic level. Two complementary minuets serve as the *galanteries*; the second features some curious, grumbling figures in the left hand that disturb the delicate keyboard texture. The gigue, here written in the sharp rhythm of a French overture, has a dramatic intensity that prefigures the gigue that ends the Partita No. 6, closing this relatively contained set with an emphatic gesture.

Since the nineteenth century, composers have used minor key signatures (A minor, B-flat minor, C-sharp minor, and so on—we will learn more about them when we look at *The Well-Tempered Clavier*) to identify music that expresses pain, sadness, and conflict. Indeed, when listeners hear the opening of works in minor keys, such as Beethoven's Fifth or Ninth symphonies, or the "Appassionata" sonata for piano, the darkness and turbulence of their expressive points of view are immediately obvious. But for baroque composers, minor keys did not necessarily signal gloom or struggle. The second of Bach's French Suites, in C minor, is cheerful and elegant, in the manner of French keyboard music, as are a number of other works by the composer in the same key, including the second Toccata and the Partita No. 2, and the second Prelude and Fugue from Book I of *The Well-Tempered Clavier.*

The second French Suite opens with an allemande in which a graceful, long-spun melody sways above a bass line that ambles along easily below. Bach adds rhythmic interest with a middle voice enlivened by the placing of emphases on unexpected beats, which he here accomplishes by holding notes for longer than the ear expects. The second half of the two-part dance is more richly ornamented and busier, with lots of little notes decorating the melody, yet the composer keeps the textures transparent. As we shall see, this movement also anticipates the opening movement of the second Partita. A vigorous courante follows, with its characteristic stabbing upbeats, and some playful rhythmic distortion in the second half that may confuse the first-time listener's ear. In the end, Bach brings the pulse back into normal focus. In keeping with the lighter tone of the Suite, the sarabande seems passionate without brooding tragically like some of the others. Its beautiful melody has an operatic affect, a sort of emotional mask put on for the purpose of this serious movement, then cast off when it's over. First of the *galanteries*, the "air" that follows, has a misleading name: this is no singable "aria"; rather, a jaunty, instrumentally conceived tune that moves rapidly from hand to hand in rushing notes. A simple minuet in two parts leads to the final gigue, with a jumpy rhythmic figure that is hard to get out of the head. A couple of passionate outbursts in shorter notes deepen the tone of this charming suite just before the end.

The second English Suite, in A minor, opens with a long, animated movement in a driving rhythm that seems far more Italian than English or French. At times the voices come together in powerful chordal figures that sound like the tutti sections (the parts when soloist and orchestra play together) of a string concerto by Vivaldi; a climax and a pause for breath two-thirds of the way through is reminiscent of a toccata. Bach's counterpoint here consists mostly of two parts, but he adds a third and fourth voice as expressive needs arise: his polyphony here is fairly free. The dreamy melancholy of the allemande is typical of the species, but the gorgeous courante is one of the composer's most splendid for the keyboard. Interweaving, serpentine lines mark the intense second half. The sarabande reaches for the tragic with its breadth and emotional impact, and is notable musically for falling melodic sequences, and harmonic richness. The score contains a lavishly decorated, written-out variation, marked "*Les agréments de la même Sarabande*"—"the ornaments for the same sarabande." A pair of complementary bourrées follows. Simple in texture but rhythmically driving, they wake the listener (and the player!) after the dreamy, slow sarabande. The final gigue continues in their mood, with a skipping rhythm but earnest force that provides an uncompromising ending to this serious suite.

With the opening Prélude of the third English Suite, in G minor, Bach takes even further his experimentation with concerto-like forms and keyboard writing, foreshadowing the Italian Concerto (CD Tracks 10, 11, and 12) of nearly two decades later. This brilliant movement is a bold experiment, even for this daring composer. It might help to compare it with the first movement of a concerto for two violins by Vivaldi, because it opens with a Vivaldi-like passage in which the parts, each played by a separate finger, enter in rapid succession, quickly building up a thick texture and an impressive sonority. Impossible to ignore, too, is the powerful forward thrust of the three-beat rhythm that dominates the movement, and with Bach captures the essence of the Italian style and feeling. The big chords that jump from one hand to the other mimic the sound of the orchestra in a concerto, whereas the lighter-textured passages represent the sound of the imaginary soloist or soloists, with the figuration in the right hand being a convincing imitation of Vivaldi's busy violin style. The massive passage that follows is much like a baroque concerto's "development" section, the solo instrument or instruments and the orchestra trading thematic material. The forceful opening rhythm returns, as the music drives joyfully ahead—this being another example of a piece in a minor key dominated by a dancelike energy rather than conflict or sorrow. Bach again piles up the sonorities as the movement pushes with ever increasing brilliance and force to its conclusion. When you listen, pay attention to the fantastic writing for the left hand in superb imitation of the basso continuo section (the instruments that guide the rhythm and harmony) of a baroque string orchestra. Huge in scale, texture, and ambition, this imitation of a concerto grosso for keyboard represents a magnificent imaginative leap.

Bach returns for the rest of the suite to the French style, beginning with the suave allemande, which features a gracefully drooping bass line in its first section, and parallel languorous closing phrases to end both. The courante has great energy but a delicacy in the keyboard writing as well. The brooding sarabande looks ahead to Chopin in its use of the deeper tones of the instrument in a persuasive impression of a cello. As in the previous suite, this sarabande comes with its own densely embroidered variation. The composer thins the texture considerably and punches up the rhythm for the marvelous twinned gavottes, the first of which has the left hand repeat notes in an unusual and rustic gesture from the sophisticated and harmonically restless Bach; the second is a delicious musette, or bagpipe imitation, complete with a long-held, droning note in the left hand. A fugal gigue of high energy concludes this grand and grandly scaled suite.

The contrast between the large scale and virile energy of the third English Suite with the inward-looking, delicate French Suite No. 3, in B minor, could hardly be greater. The beautiful allemande with which this suite opens is a wonderful example of Bach's melancholy, verging even on the sorrowful. Even the opening notes, broken into three instead of the more direct single note usual for this form, suggest a sigh. But the three-note figure dominates this tightly organized movement, appearing again and again in the opening measures, and no fewer than ten times in the three-bar passage that follows. Lovely, too, are the slower falling notes, one for every two in the right, in the left hand. Enjoy listening to the long, winding phrases of the gorgeous closing phrase, in which Bach finds one last, graceful turn. The two-part writing is of absolute clarity throughout. The second part mirrors the first, inverting the sighing figure, which dominates as obsessively here as it did the first half; the phrase of longer notes also takes a large role. Note how, just before the end, the two voices wind down together in another long, dreamy closing phrase that leaves the web of this magical movement unbroken.

To shatter inevitably the mood of this fine-spun tone poem comes the courante, which, though sharp in comparison with the allemande, is a fairly delicate example of its species as well. The upward-reaching opening phrase of the sarabande evokes once more the meditative mood of the opening, then in the second half Bach gives the lower voice a long, passionate phrase that again anticipates Chopin's admirable use of a similar sonority in several works, notably the Étude in C-sharp Minor, Op. 25, No. 7. Singular in the dance suites among the *galanteries,* at least in name, is the anglaise that follows; a little ironic, too, that it landed in a "French" suite rather than an "English" one. (Remember that those are not the composer's own names.) This charming movement, otherwise a standard two-part dance in a two-beat meter, has a briskness that makes it sound very much like a bourrée or a gavotte. This movement has a bite not heard before in this moody suite, to which the strong rhythm, pungent harmony, and sharp melodic profile all contribute, and which the succeeding pair of minuets perpetuates. By the time we hear the gigue, which is of course in a more urgent rhythm, Bach has changed the mood of the suite from melancholy to something more energetic, though he maintains to the end the gossamer fabric of this magical suite—which is perhaps just a bit neglected among these works.

With the opening allemande of the fourth French Suite, in E-flat major, we seem to be in a different world. There is a feeling of amplitude where in the previous suite everything was reduced to its essence, and the fat sound and richness of three voices takes the place of two. Bach renders the top voice as arpeggios—chords broken apart and played as individual notes, a device used constantly by composers of works for the keyboard. Long notes sound far below in the bass, as the third voice works the middle between the two. This movement has a sound most characteristic of the composer working on the clavier in this tonality, as the arpeggiated notes float grandly around the rest, creating a rich, hazy timbre. The opening section of the Prélude, Fugue and Allegro (see chapter 9, page 109) has a very similar sound, as does the E-flat major prelude from Book I of *The Well-tempered Clavier*. Bach clearly liked the combinations. The composer plays with rhythms in the courante, having the right hand play the melody, a nearly steady stream of triplets against dotted notes (long, then short) in the left. Instead of being a dark sarabande, this example seems bathed in light, without the composer's sacrificing a bit of the usual heaven-gazing sublimity to which this form always inspires him. And Bach now continues to expand the scope of his suites, here including three *galanterie* movements: a gavotte that is both chunkier and more expansive than any comparable movement in the first three French Suites, a brief but utterly charming minuet, and a two-voice air similar in style to the one in the second of this series, quick and energetic, with a running figure, played mostly by the right hand, set against bouncing rhythms in the left. The gigue, with its lilting rhythm and rustic feel, suggests the horns of a hunting scene.

The Prélude of the fourth English Suite, in F major, opens chastely with a reminiscence of a two-part invention, but within a few moments the concerto-like textures of the previous English Suite return. This huge movement is considerably longer, if rather less forceful, than its energetic predecessor. It's also the only piece in any of the suite, English or French, to which Bach gives a tempo indication, *vitement*—"rapidly"—in French, of course. Here his style is suave, as voices (up to four) enter as he needs them then drop out until recalled. Thus, the two-part texture dominates the proceedings, as the composer takes his rolling theme, sonata-like, through a rainbow of keys. Here Bach works on a scale considerably larger than in any preceding movement in the sets we've examined so far. This remarkable Prélude ends, about six minutes without repeats after it begins, in the same calm mood and elegant style with which it began.

Ornate, mellow, and apparently cheerful, the first section of the allemande is dominated by the sound of trills and triplets. But Bach soon takes his theme through some harmonic detours, a maneuver not unusual for him that also deepens and complicates the second half of the dance considerably. Here, as usual, the theme is inverted, making ambiguous what first seemed straightforward and amiable. Gracefulness and genuine good spirits, however, dominate the courante that follows. The sarabande introduces a meditative note, while continuing the harmonic richness that was made evident earlier in the suite. Both halves end with a strikingly rich phrase in parallel notes; and sophisticated as it is, the entire movement feels like one of the Bach's improvisations at the keyboard captured on paper. In this way it looks ahead to the sarabande of the Partita No. 1. Two minuets serve as *galanteries,* with the exquisite second, in a cool D minor, casting a shadow, slight but refreshing.

The final gigue opens with a scampering hunting-horn call similar to that of final dance of the fourth French Suite, but delicately idealized rather than earthy; then in the second half, Bach as usual inverts the theme, making it sound strange, and adds a sequence of bumping notes an octave apart that create a more rustic effect, more typical of a hunting theme. But in this movement, as in the allemande and the sarabande, the second parts of these two-part dances are more complex than the first. Add to these the hugely proportioned Prélude, and we have a work that, while basically upbeat, is large in scale and far from simple.

In the fifth English Suite, in E minor, Bach follows the pattern of the fourth, by opening the set with a big Prélude. But few passages in the fifth suite's first movement imitate the give-and-take of a concerto.

Instead, the movement has a lovely, swaying motion that makes it resemble a passepied, though it is far longer and more ambitious than that usually brief dance. And its mood—in fact, the mood of the entire suite—seems shaded by wistfulness, eased by the light rhythm. The movement opens with a carefully sculpted and memorable theme stated by one voice joined by a second and third, put through its paces in free counterpoint, then brought gently to its conclusion. In between, however, sequences of light chords that accentuate the dancelike feel move easily from hand to hand. The sadness is more pronounced in the allemande, another delicate example of that dance in which the voices intertwine and Bach once more steers the harmony away from the expected and commonplace. And again, its second half, pregnant with the harmonic waywardness of the first, is yet stranger and more inward.

Although the courante looks in the score like those of the other English Suites, its tone seems restrained for the normally sharp-edged dance. The beautiful melody of the sarabande (vaguely reminiscent of "Greensleeves") sounds as though inspired by an old dance. It even seems to share a dark kinship with the *Goldberg* theme.

The *Passepied en rondeau* and *Passepied II* form a magical pair, seemingly fragile, but, typically with Bach, made of material with great tensile strength. The first title means that the passepied is in rondo rather than two-part form, with its opening phrase coming back several times and at the end of the piece; the second piece follows the more common pattern. The melody is stated at the outset of the first piece, in the dainty gait normal for of the passepied. That mincing rhythm, heard in the left hand at the beginning, then throughout the dance, is typical of this form. The second passepied provides contrast in several ways to the preceding dance: first, it's in E major, sounding bright as juxtaposed to its companion; its keyboard writing is thicker, and the rhythm less emphatic. Finally, as noted, in it Bach returns to the binary form. As is normal with paired dances such as these, the *Passepied en rondeau* is repeated, turning these slender dances into a satisfying musical sandwich.

The downward slips and slides and full-on fugal treatment of the chromatic theme of the gigue show the composer in an altogether more somber state of mind, banishing the wistfulness of the suite's earlier movements. Gruff chords tug at the texture and mood at the end of the first section; even when transferred to higher notes in the right hand toward the end of the second part, they cannot alter the sense of grim urgency with which the suite ends. This dramatic final dance pulls the interesting English Suite No. 5 away from pastoral and closer to tragedy.

Although Bach intended no deliberate contrast, the fifth of the French Suites could hardly differ more, at least in mood and tone. Since there is no prelude, the French Suite No. 5, in G major, opens directly with the sweet tune of a sunny allemande. But Bach can never resist the pull of complexity, and within seconds notes foreign to G major have entered; in no time he flirts openly with G minor. But here the shadows cast by faraway sharps and flats and the tonic minor key are not "sad"; rather, they enrich the music with a rainbow of sonic color. The left-hand voices, also unusually rich, also add heft to the gorgeous textures of the movement. As always, the second part of this bipartite dance is darker in harmony and denser in material than the first. Note, when you listen, the little three-note figure in the left hand that Bach employs repeatedly to kick the motion of the dance along. The courante is a lively, affectionate takeoff on a rustic dance, in which a sawing figuration (mostly in the right hand) lovingly imitates the playing of a country fiddler. A sarabande in G major evokes in this composer a fervent, spiritual dance; the one here and that on which the *Goldberg Variations* is based have a resemblance anyone can hear, even though their bass lines differ slightly. The harmonic rhythm—the progress from G major through D major, E minor, then back home to G major—is identical but expected (that is how the form works) and the right-hand voices—the melody lines—are quite comparable. And the ecstatic tone both share is unmistakable.

Resist if you can the charming gavotte. The bourrée that follows is equally delicious. But the majestic *loure* (CD Track 3) is another matter, a dance in an immense rhythm reminiscent perhaps of a slowed-down gigue, or a sarabande with greater swing and forward motion. The term for this bit of choreography, rare outside music by French composers, comes from a small bagpipe of the same name and the slow jig danced to it,[6] audible the snapping rhythm, sharply falling phrases (0:01, 0:04, 0:10...) and the sweet drone of the cadences (0:07, 0:16, 0:36)—some positively Monteverdian in their spaciousness and gravity—in Bach's sublime takeoff. The left hand displays throughout a soulful animation that far exceeds that of basic part writing: listen to the lines at 0:21, 0:27, and 1:45 through 1:57. Listen also to the breadth and grandeur of the melodic phrases throughout. This is the only *loure* in the keyboard suites, although here is another extraordinary example in the Partita No. 3 for Violin, in E major. (Hint to the reader: listen to that one, too!) Bach's are, naturally, quite studied in their formality and refinement, owing little of their idealized French style to Highland or Irish jigs. Nevertheless, the family resemblance among them all is surprisingly clear.

Like its opposite number among the English, this set ends with a fast fugue in the form of a gigue. Its joyful mood is obvious, but the pace and force of the dance are furious, even Dionysian, on the wild side for Bach, who invariably keeps his material under tight control. Italian influence is also clear in this tarantella-like dance, which is also the most difficult movement to play in the French Suites. It supplies a rollicking conclusion to this magnificent suite.

Like the courante of the Fifth French Suite, the allemande that opens the sixth and last of the series, in E major, Bach asks the clavier to imitate the sound of another instrument. Here the leisurely figuration in the right hand might be heard as violin-like; but one might just as easily discern in the swarm of little notes that soon follow an affectionate parody of the flute. The entire first half also has a kind of innocence, more readily associated with the woodwind than the hard-edged, all-purpose sound of the fiddle, but in any case, it is surely one or the other of these agile treble instruments that Bach mimics. The theme presented at the beginning ambles along genially, with the composer's clear two-part writing enhancing the sense of ease and almost angelic composure. There is some charming rhythmic business for the lower voice halfway through the second section, after which, duetlike, the upper voice takes the rhythmic figure and the melody, broken into busy ornamental patterns, moves to the lower voice—the left hand. The second half of the dance is, as always, more complex than the first, but of all the French Suite allemandes, this is the one in which mood and tone—in this case, a profound sweetness—are unbroken from start to finish.

A flurry of fast notes help this swift-moving courante live up to its name, making it sound more like running than dancing. A sense of freedom, suggested by bold harmonic shifts right at the beginning, give the sarabande (like several others) a sense of the composer's improvising at his instrument, then writing his ideas down. This movement, like the opening allemande, is lavishly ornamented, with some expressive runs assigned to the left hand. This is the French Suite most generously endowed by Bach with *galanteries,* in this case four. First comes a charming gavotte, the sharp tune and quick tempo of which give it an edginess common to the dance. Next comes a polonaise, referred to in some editions as a *menuet polonais.* This tiny dance bears no resemblance to Chopin's mighty works of the same name. For Bach, working well before the era of musical nationalism, it is another chance to write a little character piece to fill out the set. The composer may have taken a stab at an exotic "Eastern" effect, with its odd, wiggly figuration and occasionally rude harmonies. But it's probably best to think of this polonaise through the lens of its alternative title, "Polish minuet." The real minuet (sometimes called *petit menuet*) sounds suave in contrast to the polonaise, but a curious tic—a four-note rhythmic figure in the left hand—tugs steadily at the lyrical melodic line and delicate texture of the dance. Like the gavotte, the energetic bourrée adds a jolt of melody and rhythm, intimately bound, to the proceedings. The clean, two-part texture gives this more rustic dance a sense that Bach is copying artfully the sound of two players (a piper and a bass player) at a county dance. As in the previous suite, the gigue is fast, joyous, and fugal in style.

Last and longest of the English Suites, the sixth, in D minor, is conceived on a huge scale, approaching the biggest of the Partitas— the fourth and the sixth—in length and scope. Its grandiose opening movement exceeds those of all the partitas in length and playing time. The remaining movements, even the *galanteries,* share the spaciousness and depth of the Prélude—and its character, sometimes nightmarish, and even demonic. So ahead of its period in tone is this astonishing work that Bach seems to foreshadow composers of the late classical school, notably Beethoven and Schubert, and it is no stretch to hear in its freedom and boldness the style of some of Schumann's greatest piano works.

Formally the Prélude is a fantasia, with toccata-like features. The sweeping arpeggios of the opening page form a long introductory passage that suggests, like many of these movements, an improvisation written down. The main themes of the movement are these arpeggios, a dancelike theme that springs from them, a hopping rhythmic figure that resembles the accompaniment to a passepied, and a theme built of repeated notes, pecked at thoughtfully. After the opening sequence, rich in harmony and troubled in mood, there is a brief, expressive pause on a ripe, melodic turn—marked *adagio*—that seems as though lifted directly from one of the toccatas. The dancelike theme then emerges above a swirling, accelerated accompaniment presented earlier in fragmentary form, and throbbing syncopations appear in the left hand. The pecking figure appears, seeming calm and almost meditative amid the turbulence, and richly harmonized melodic fragments soar above the themes, which the composer pulls apart and blends artfully as the various come and go like troubled dreams: there is no mistaking the darkness behind the music, intensely lyrical though it is. Sometimes Bach thins the texture, as though pulling back from his most turbulent ideas, but at others the keyboard writing is dense and dark-hued. The music sweeps forcefully toward an ending that surprises with in its laconic suddenness. This is not Bach's most tightly organized work, but it is profound, beautiful, and profoundly disturbing.

The allemande makes a quiet postscript to the dark ruminations of the opening section. Its theme is decorated by a turn Bach repeats almost obsessively. The harmony is rich but somber. A brief, intense courante follows. Listen for the strange, tormented convolutions to which the composer subjects the melodic line. A sarabande with a double (remember: a variation) follows. In this exalted soliloquy Bach does not stray from the troubled tone he has adopted; the variation has a more flowing character than the dance itself, but keeps to the same. Some broken chords toward its end recall the grand arpeggios that opened the Prélude.

Two gavottes take the tough role of *galanteries* in this tragic work. But these are two of the finest Bach wrote (CD Track 4). The brisk rhythm of the first lighten the mood after the brooding sarabande but menace lurks below its trim and tidy surface. Utterly Schumann-esque—and like his wildest works: the *Davidsbündlertänze* and *Kreisleriana*—are the shortened, spooky cadence at 1:19 that ends the first gavotte, and the long, drifting sequence from 0:46 to 0:59. The second, a droning musette (2:15), seems a shockingly forward-looking voice from heaven anticipating Schubert, Schumann, and even Mahler. Note the strange, dreamy, flickering trill at 3:02, repeated at 3:35. There are of course few more effective ways for an artist to intensify the depth of the surrounding gloom, and the distance of hope, than to isolate a line of light in the middle of that darkness.

The terrifying gigue, the dark sibling of the one that ends the G major French Suite, also anticipates many wild, hopeless, dance-of-death finales, like the finales of Beethoven's Sonata in D minor, Op. 31 No. 2 (the "Tempest"); Schubert's C minor Piano Sonata, his String Quartets in D minor and G major; of the finale of Chopin's Sonata in B-flat Minor and several of the Preludes, and perhaps even that of Berlioz's *Symphonie fantastique*. One need only listen carefully to its snarling trills, slippery chromatic harmonic scheme, and short, sharp, dissonant chords to perceive the long shadow it casts over the romantic-demonic style.

The Well-Tempered Clavier, *Book I*

The bland, curious, catchall title of *The Well-Tempered Clavier* hardly suggests the variety and power of its music. Nor does the second level of description add much: a collection of forty-eight preludes and fugues, in two volumes. These, the composer gathered and organized over the course of many years and published in collections of twenty-four each, the first in 1722, and the second twenty years later.

This cornerstone of Western music began as a tool for Bach to teach his gifted eldest son keyboard technique and composition. Some of the pieces appeared in original form in the *Clavier-Büchlein*—the "Little Clavier Book"—for Wilhelm Friedemann. Others were composed later, specifically for *The Well-Tempered Clavier,* though many in the second volume also came into being as instructional pieces for a later generation of Bach's students.

In any case, the dry-sounding "preludes and fugues" says next to nothing about the wide range of musical styles and the energy of the pieces contained in these collections. A *prelude* suggests only a piece that precedes another; a *fugue* is, of course, a contrapuntal process subject to a variety of complex rules. But here Bach's preludes are as important and expressive as his fugues. Many of these preludes are technical studies, designed to develop the player's skills—each focusing, as Chopin's would a century later, on a different mechanical problem facing keyboard players. Most are also character pieces, which means that they portray a single mood, or emotion—what baroque musicians referred to as an *affect*. Yet again this makes the music sound dry: these technical studies and character pieces are tender, wild, fantastical, passionate, furious, and comical. Many are brilliant, toccata-like movements, very hard to play.

The Well-Tempered Clavier and Its Title

The peculiar title begs the question: what does *well-tempered* mean? Of course *clavier* refers broadly to keyboard instruments. Bach found it important to mention tempering—an aspect of tuning—in the title because adequate tuning in all the two dozen standard keys on one keyboard instrument was not taken for granted. Before the eighteenth century, keyboard instruments other than organs were inconsistent in this respect, playing well in three or four closely related keys, then moderately so in a few more, but far out of tune in the rest. *Tempering* refers to a way of tuning of the instrument, be it harpsichord, clavichord, or the earliest pianos, so that all twenty-four keys—C major, B-flat minor, and the rest—sound good. But it's not a synonym: the title doesn't merely mean "the well-tuned keyboard."

Perfect tuning is impossible to achieve, but over the years many systems arose to regulate and refine the process. By the 1600s, musicians worked more and more with the twelve notes now in use, and they, alongside instrument builders, developed methods of shaving some of the inequalities inherent to tuning, thus evening out—*tempering*—painful-sounding little differences. That way, all twenty-four keys, based on the dozen notes we know, each one sprouting a major and a minor key, sound good to most ears. This tuning system, which now dominates musical practice, is called *equal temperament*. The musical tones we know are, therefore, slightly corrupt versions of an ideal but unattainable harmony. Composers such as Chopin and Wagner fully exploited the tonal rainbows implicit in the twelve-note system and equal temperament tuning; twentieth-century composers, such as Debussy, Stravinsky, Schoenberg, and their successors based their music on the absolute equality of the twelve tones.

This is an interesting but recondite subject: math, physics, acoustics, and philosophy as well as music influenced the development of the twelve-note and equal temperament systems. Those interested in learning more might read Stuart Isacoff's 2001 book *Temperament*. Controversy over whether equal temperament tuning is right for all music continues, too: Ross Duffin's more technical *How Equal Temperament Ruined Harmony* (2007) revisits the story from a different point of view, noting that many distinguished performers dislike the one-size-fits-all nature of equal temperament, and asks whether that system is the right approach for all performance.

What does all this have to do with Bach and his two grand cycles of preludes and fugues? As the most sophisticated musical technician of his time, Bach probably accepted the equality of the twenty-four keys available to him through equal temperament tuning. He composed *The Well-Tempered Clavier* at least in part to explore all the keys, in the process creating what the pianist and musicologist Charles Rosen described as "a monument to the ambiguity of tonal relations."[1] Wanda Landowska wrote earlier in a similar vein that some of the fugues "seem to glorify the victory of equal temperament."[2] In his study of *The Well-Tempered Clavier,* David Ledbetter speculates reasonably that Bach moved in steps toward equal temperament over the course of his career. But this is a tricky and controversial topic, and ultimately it's best to heed Ledbetter's warning: "We have no way of knowing what Bach's exact tuning preferences were."[3]

The term *fugue* is surely intimidating and dry, too, but Bach's are extraordinary conceptions, in which the composer shows his mastery of the process; like the preludes, the fugues express wildly disparate, powerful emotions, held in check by the reins of the composer's intellectual rigor. A crucial aspect of these fugues is how some display Bach's interest in what is called the *stile antico,* Italian for the "old style" of counterpoint. Here the composer looks back to Renaissance polyphony for inspiration, writing many of the greatest fugues in the manner of a century or more before his time. Thus, when listening, for example, to the B-flat minor fugue (or the C-sharp minor, the D-sharp minor, or the F-sharp minor) in Book I, what you hear is a backward-looking, self-consciously learned style of part writing, which Bach carries off with complete success. In this way he acts much as later composers would when dropping into fugal writing (though rarely as persuasively) often in tribute to Bach. Other fugues are in a more modern, choreographic, light-textured style, known as *galant,* in fashion at the time. Still others, notably the B minor fugue that closes Book I, look to the future.

The Well-Tempered Clavier would have been too much as a teaching tool for Bach's own students of composition: "For young composers especially, the *WTC* is more a Counsel of Perfection than a practical book of instruction."[4] But for great composers who followed, most of whom played one sort of keyboard or another, it stood as perhaps the most powerful influence, though not always a healthy one. Some composers, such as Schubert, lacked a feel for counterpoint. When, for example, this otherwise extraordinary composer tried awkwardly to write the finale of the popular *Wanderer Fantasy* in fugal form, he needed to retreat almost immediately. Others, such as Beethoven and Schumann, adapted Bach with mixed results, doing best when not trying too hard to copy him literally. Others—particularly Haydn, Mozart, and Chopin—metabolized Bach's lessons efficiently, putting them to the most brilliant use by adapting what they'd learned from his counterpoint to their own creative idioms. And in the middle of the last century, in open homage to Bach, Dmitri Shostakovich wrote a set of twenty-four brilliant preludes and fugues that successfully reflected the Russian's own skittish, ironic style.

Another influence on Bach in writing "the Forty-eight" was the development during his lifetime of keyboard tuning systems that made all twenty-four keys available in a practical way. He may not have been the first composer to work in rare key signatures, but he was unquestionably the first great one to do it; and it seems likely that the form of *The Well-Tempered Clavier* clarified itself in his mind as his work on it progressed. Encyclopedic by nature and intellectually ambitious, Bach began this as a mundane project to produce material to teach his son, but it turned into a complete study of the newly available keys and how to compose in them, in Christoph Wolff's words, "not merely to teach others but to challenge himself."[5] In this sense it falls into the category of his other comprehensive projects, which among others include such titanic creations at the Sonatas and Partitas for solo violin, the suites for solo cello, the *St. Matthew Passion,* and *The Art of the Fugue.*

The characters of musical keys—the named tonalities such as C major, A minor, and so on—was and remains a subject of discussion and controversy. Keys have been assigned moods and affects; for example, "E major has a very common eighteenth century association with blessedness...."[6] For musicians and music lovers, some of these impressions ring strangely true, many seem ridiculous, and ultimately all are subjective. Certainly some keys—D minor and E-flat major, for instance—seem with some consistency to suggest to Bach certain types of thematic ideas, figuration, and affects, but it's probably best to leave this soft and speculative issue to musical historians.

Be that as it may, it seems wise to keep in mind when listening to *The Well-Tempered Clavier* its original, didactic purpose: these pieces were written for teaching and private study; pianists' custom of playing one volume or the other in recital seems questionable, as the recital form didn't even exist until a century after Bach's death; and the tough, tight complexity and intimate nature of *The Well-Tempered Clavier* makes for difficult listening in a big concert hall. Genuinely careful attention to this detailed, intense music seems limited for ordinary mortals to a few: three or four, but surely no more than six preludes and fugues at a time are plenty for us to chew on. As concentration is harder at the end of the day, after dinner, a recital—however fine—is often tough going. Finally, there is the question of performance: it takes a really remarkable performer to carry him- or herself as well as an audience through a full evening of twenty-four. That said, each paired prelude and fugue should be heard together, as Bach designed them to be. It's far better to hear to one pair well than to drowse pointlessly through more than you can take in.

Thus, listeners should always remember that *The Well-Tempered Clavier* is private music, conceived for study, practice, and listening in small, considered doses, alone or in small groups:

> The *Well-Tempered Keyboard,* while effective enough in the modern concert hall, was not composed for an audience but for the pleasure and instruction of the performer: any public performance is certain to leave the audience in the dark about the many aspects of the work perceptible only to the performer, who sees them in the score, and above all feels them through the muscles of his hand and arm.[7]

The first prelude and fugue, in the supposedly neutral key of C major, are among the best known. The prelude consists of an even-flowing stream of arpeggios, two per bar, in which Bach makes exquisitely calculated tonal shifts to reveal a rainbow of rich harmonies. Yet under his tight management, the steady flow of the material is artfully reined in. The piece has an unmistakable prefatory quality, working surprisingly well as opener to this vast and complex series, given its modest scale and contained keyboard range—Bach keeps the music mostly within a very narrow compass of notes. Perhaps it is the work's harmonic breadth that gives the sense of horizons that are opening. It also has a fresh sound, as if it is an improvisation, though of course that sense is yet another example of Bach's art.

Its influence on other composers has been enormous: Chopin, for example, opens his first set of Études, Op. 10, and the Preludes, Op. 28, with surging pieces in C major, both modeled on this; "From Foreign Lands and People," the first piece of Schumann's *Scenes from Childhood,* Op. 15, is another broken chord study that shows Bach's influence in its textures and expectant tone. In *Danseuses de Delphes,* the prelude that opens the first book of Debussy's two great sets, the chords remain unbroken, but their lines cross beautifully in a way that makes the source of that master's inspiration clear; Debussy, too, appreciated and captured Bach's prefatory tone. Finally, Charles Gounod tampered disgracefully with perfection by using Bach's two-page masterwork as the accompaniment for his aria "Ave Maria," adding to it a treacly melodic overlay.

Following this evocative opening meditation is a difficult job, which Bach dispatches triumphantly with a glorious, four-voice sequence based on a steady, rising subject. Notable for the density of its textures, this majestic four-voiced fugue contains many stretti—entries of the theme that come close together, continually intensifying the music. And, after the density and power of the counterpoint, the music trails off, as though heavenward, in a rising figure set against a dramatically thinned texture. "Just as drawings are often sketches of paintings, so are many of the fugues suggestions of choral works";[8] harpsichordist and Bach scholar Ralph Kirkpatrick noted; this grandiose fugue seems a good example of what Kirkpatrick meant.

The second prelude and fugue, in C minor (CD Tracks 5 and 6), are as well known as the opening pair, and, in their very different ways, just as great. Here, a fierce rhythmic drive replaces the gentle undulations of the C major prelude, and in place of the upward gaze of the C major fugue, its C minor sibling is a worldly and intoxicating dance.

Note from the outset the density of the keyboard texture of the toccata-like prelude, which bursts with fantastic energy and excitement and bristles with edgy and beautiful dissonance. The roiling, boiling texture remains unchanged from the opening notes through to 0:54, but note at 0:40 how Bach twists the lines dramatically by changing their direction. He calls on the player to do ever more finger-twisting stuff from here to the end; at 0:54 the two hands break apart to share a single, intense thematic line. At 1:02, the composer gives the tempo instruction *presto,* quick, as the lines again intertwine and race ahead; starting at 1:07, some strangely beautiful harmonies flash by. The player's fingers must shift directions three times in the three bars from 1:11 to 1:15, as the pattern breaks fiercely on rolled chords interspersed by fast, passionate passagework (marked *adagio*) (1:15 to 1:24). This wildly exciting piece ends in moody grandeur as Bach broadens the harmony, pulling into C major at the very end.

Listeners love the C minor fugue, in three voices, for its grace and good cheer, but its virile energy matches that of the prelude. The joyous subject, in a choreographic short-short-long rhythm the composer used often, enters at the outset, answered at 0:06. The falling figure in slower notes in the right hand at 0:18 is the countersubject, as the counterpoint develops around five episodes (the first at 0:22) at its center. At 0:40, the left hand takes over, driving the contrapuntal structure ahead; at 1:13, it delivers the subject once again. With the final phrase, at 1:21, Bach stops the bass line—the lowest thematic strand—on a long-held note called a *pedal point,* slowing the momentum above as a result. As in the prelude, Bach changes harmony rapidly, ending in C major with a rainbow of tones. This fugue is quite similar thematically and in character to the concluding section of the Sinfonia of the C minor Partita, and to one of the central sections of the Toccata in the same key. Clearly this was a musical idea that had a hold on the composer.

C-sharp major, the key of the next prelude and fugue, has seven sharps in its signature, as many as a tonality can have; it's played mostly on the black keys and sounds as though its feet aren't on the ground. C-sharp major has always been rare and was otherwise unheard of in

Bach's day. So this pair is interesting for its remarkable quality and high spirits, and also for the composer's daring in making it work, although doing so was, of course, just a part of his methodical exploration of the twenty-four keys.

The prelude opens in with quick, even notes above a delicate dance rhythm reminiscent of a passepied; it is playful, even kittenish. The second half of this short but delicious movement consists of a kind of broken chord known at the time by the French word *batterie*. An arpeggio sweeps up the keyboard, then down, and the piece ends on three guitarlike chords. More than one knowledgeable commentator has heard in this music the influence of Spanish music and Bach's magnificent contemporary Domenico Scarlatti, the Italian master of keyboard who worked in Spain: "It is certain that Bach was familiar with Scarlatti's sonatas and admired them."[9] Beneath the lightness and charm of the music, and giving it grip, lie Bach's taut workmanship and characteristic rhythmic drive.

The three-part fugue in C-sharp major is based on a glittering subject, with big jumps, that sounds like a birdsong. Not a shadow passes over this joyful, fast-moving fugue, which is very difficult to play. Landowska, whose technical mastery sounds impregnable, wrote movingly, "How many days of unrelenting work, of deprivation, of indescribable efforts to succeed in playing with insouciance, with careless ease. Fugue III, for example."[10]

With the grand fourth prelude and fugue, in C-sharp minor, Bach brings us to the first climactic piece in Book I. These stand as well among the biggest and most powerful of the entire series. The key signature was one he, like most baroque composers, used rarely. By Beethoven's time, it had become more common; Schumann used it frequently; and it is unquestionably one of Chopin's favorite keys. As for the prelude, it has been described as an aria (like the sarabande that is the *Goldberg* theme); a slowed-down courante, and more likely a means for a player to develop an expressive, cantabile (songlike) style than a technique-building study, like the first three. The main theme consists of a graceful, six-note falling figure, followed by a mournful rise. Moving at a moderate pace, it has a dancelike lilt but a weary, melancholy affect, too. Some players ornament the work generously, whereas others prefer to let the melodic line speak for itself; both inter-pretive approaches work.

The gravity of the first subject, coming out of the bass, make it dif-ficult to escape the tragic portent of the massive, five-voiced fugue in the *stile antico*. Yet Bach allows rays of light to enter, in the form of the more flowing second subject, in steady eighth notes. Technically it is an remarkable display, with its three interweaving subjects of varied character, and a *periodic structure*, which means that Bach divides it into sections, perceptible to the ear yet seamlessly interwoven. But in any case, it's best initially to listen to this solemn fugue for its grandeur and expressivity.

The contrast in tone between the gravity of the C-sharp minor fugue and the comical tone and light texture of the prelude in D major is as great as could be. For Bach, D major was often the key for rejoicing, but this quirky étude, although cheerful enough—is not in that vein. Resembling a toccata in its perpetual motion, the bumpy bass line (the left-hand part) of this witty technical study jumps about more mani-cally than does the busy figuration of the right, which somehow seems as though it is always scrambling to keep up with those leaps in the left. Excitement builds as the movement progresses, and Bach introduces in the bass a pedal point that starts to pull the disparate elements together. The hands finally move in tandem; then suddenly the composer changes the tone markedly with a big chords that surround a long, rather grand flourish. These set the stage for the four-voice fugue, only twenty-seven bars long but big in character.

And the character is that of a French overture, the grandiose form Bach crams, with perhaps a touch of satire, into two pages. But every-thing is there from the rushing scales, to the stark dotted rhythms, and the feeling of pomp and pride. The fugue ends on a chord sequence of genuine grandeur. This short but stunning fugue seems far closer in its compression to Variation 16 of the *Goldbergs* than to the spacious opening movement of the fourth Partita, another French overture in D major (CD Track 8).

Fast moving and intense, the D minor prelude represents yet another study in playing broken chords, with the melody embedded into the figuration. The bass lines pulses relentlessly throughout, giving the piece a feverish impetus. But the fine-boned texture remains mostly in two parts, until Bach decides to call in a third; the work is daring harmonically, with many unresolved dissonances in the chain of broken chords in the right hand just before the powerful final cadence. This prelude, although only twenty-six bars long and ninety seconds in playing time, is a remarkable example of the composer's ability to create a nightmarish affect and hold his material under the tightest possible rein, all while effecting an flawless study of an aspect of keyboard technique. Every commentator seems to mention the aggressive character of the companion fugue, from its theme that arches like a threatening cobra, to its snatched notes, to the snarling trills that add to its menacing character.

The prelude and fugue in E-flat major make a fascinating pair, the grand proportions and stately pace of the opening section contrasting markedly with the brief, babbling three-part fugue. But observant commentators have noted that the fugue contains "many subtle allusions to the material of the prelude."[11] What this means is that the attentive listener will make the connections, without necessarily knowing what they are, or even that they exist. The point is that there's greater unity between the two than is initially apparent—Bach knew what he was doing. It's also worth noting that E-flat major, which has three flats in its key signature, symbolized the Trinity for Bach, the tripartite divinity and key signature apparently inspiring him to a fair number of pieces that share the sublime mood of this prelude. Perhaps closest in form and spirit to this prelude and fugue is the great, if rarely heard Prelude, Fugue, and Allegro, also in E-flat major where the composer also meditates and expounds musically on the number three.

This prelude, in three sections, opens with a calm passage in long, rolling phrases, with an improvisatory quality, which could well be how it originated. Following a flourish in the right hand, the second section enters—a fugue in slower notes—that looks backward to the serene, triumphant polyphony of Palestrina and the Flemish masters. Even though they are very different in style and movement, Bach connects them so artfully that one seems to flow from the other. The third section, which again seems to spring naturally from the slow-note fugue, is a *double fugue*, meaning it has two subjects, both of which we have heard already, though separately: the rolling theme of the opening passage and the slow note theme of the fugue that forms the second part of this grandiose triptych. This section, by far the longest of the three, is colossal in scale and profound in its spirituality. It's also different in style from the preludes that we've looked at until now, being in no sense a technical study. This is also the only prelude in *The Well-Tempered Clavier* that contains a fully worked-out fugue.[12]

The burbling theme of the companion fugue here, built of cascading figuration with a breathless pause at its center, has an unmistakable dance pulse; it also shares a joyous, birdsong quality with the subject of the C-sharp major fugue, amplified in this subject by a cheerful trill. In both fugues, Bach makes the fast notes rattle by briskly; but in this one, a long passage in the middle drops into a minor key. The pause in the subject reappears wittily in both hands right before the end. Although this quick bit of counterpoint seems to speak a different language from the long-spun, divine rhetoric of prelude, there are, as noted, many internal links, which Bach found a new way to express.

The colossal, climactic eighth prelude and fugue make one of the most gripping pairs in *The Well-Tempered Clavier*. It is unusual for a technical reason, too, in that the prelude and fugue are in the same key, but Bach notates them in different key signatures, the prelude in E-flat minor and the fugue in its *enharmonic* (differing in name only) equivalent, D-sharp minor. (E-flat and D-sharp are the same note.) As we shall see, the Book II prelude and fugue are both in D-sharp minor. It's unclear why Bach did this, but this should not interfere with one's appreciation of these dark-hued twins.

Opening with a sobbing figure in a dotted rhythm that rises above from majestic arpeggiated chords, the tragic tone of the glorious lament that is the prelude cannot be mistaken. Writhing figures that seem like an impassioned soliloquy finally coalesce, but Bach keeps them firmly in the grip of the powerful rhythm set forth by the chords. Midway through, a weird, wailing motif suggests rhythmically that a French overture style trying to take over, but the steadily flowing, gorgeous, somber chords reassert their dominance immediately. This powerful movement also may remind some of the more tragic sarabandes in the dance suites.

Don't look for consolation in the tremendous, backward-looking three-voice fugue: again, from the very opening notes, the music seems in the grip of the deepest, darkest emotions Bach can express. Although he does it using every contrapuntal device in his armory; the technical devices, which look back to Palestrina and the older compositional school, are only a means to Bach's aesthetic end. Midway through, for example, he *inverts* the theme, turning it on its head, in a titanic phrase deep in the bass that seems to ring across the universe. This is the second-longest fugue in Book I except for the last, in B minor, and one of the most potent and profound in *The Well-Tempered Clavier*.

The key of E major consistently elicits from Bach music with a bright, cool sound (blessedness?), like that of the French Suite No. 6. This prelude and fugue follow the pattern. The prelude is a siciliano, a pastoral dance form in an irresistible, lilting rhythm. Even though the complexity-loving Bach darkens the harmony at several points, the rhythm remains soothing throughout, with quicker notes always there to certify the joyful character of this brief but satisfying dance. One longer run about two-thirds of the way through practically wiggles with happy excitement.

The three-voice fugue, which moves quickly from beginning to end, has for its subject a rising melodic figure kicked off by a strong, short-long rhythm stated in the first two notes and which dominates the texture of this bustling, witty movement. There is also a counter-subject—a second theme—that crows like a rooster.

The prelude of the E minor pair is a beauty; Bach seems to have revised it many times, from its first appearance in a teaching notebook for his son, to its final, complex form here. The right hand intones a passionate, ornate, aria-like theme over a bass line that flows steadily and hypnotically. This lyric utterance grows ever more intense, when suddenly, the music breaks into a fast-running passage in two voices marked *presto* by Bach, completely different in tone, texture, and speed from what preceded it. It's somewhat reminiscent of a parallel passage in the C minor prelude, but where that is burly and powerful, this one is startling in its windblown grace. It's a lovely, bold conception.

Singular also among the fugues is its companion piece, the only one in two voices in *The Well-Tempered Clavier*. Resembling a two-part invention, this muscular essay in dance rhythm is based on an aggressive and serpentine subject that rushes up, then falls in a sliding chromatic pattern. Bach puts it briskly through its paces; the friction of the two voices seem to give off sparks, and, like the prelude, its sound is not quite like anything else in the series. Some are put off by the fugue's wiry texture and furious speed, but it's a brilliant complement to the prelude, with Bach adopting for it the same swift pace as that movement's second part.

Buzzing trills punctuate the F major prelude that follows, and its fugue, too. The prelude, a brisk and busy two-voice toccata in a fast triplet rhythm, is marked not only by trills but by long passages of running notes, as well. Even the slowest notes, which carry the flowing melody, seem fast, and it feels over before we have a chance to appreciate is beauty and good cheer. But the long trills dominate its texture to an unusual extent. A powerful dance rhythm rules the three-part fugue, which looks on paper very much like a passepied, the lively triple-time dance used by Bach in many of his suites. As noted, the subject contains a trill, so that the fugue sounds like an extension of the prelude. The subject and development are cheerful, and the choreographic feeling unmistakable.

Bach conceives the F minor prelude and fugue that follow in extraordinary beauty and magnitude. Here the fugue, epic in size and scope, calls for a prelude that's lighter in texture, if not in mood. This beautiful prelude is a study in sustaining notes, a mark of skill in a harpsichord player. Here he breaks the chords, burying the melody in the sweeping figuration that results. The rhythm seems a bit easier here, more of a steady rocking; in the middle, Bach artfully blurs the edges of the beat further, holding notes for longer than the ear expects. But the textures throughout are of a rare delicacy, and the mood is of a slightly morbid melancholy very typical for the composer.

The gripping four-part fugue opens with a slow and winding *chromatic subject*, which means that the notes seem to slide together, rather than move stepwise, also giving the subject an ominous tone. The fugue is one of the most old-fashioned pieces in *The Well-Tempered Clavier*, sounding as though it might be a somber church motet from a century or more before. Even the tonal scheme has ties to a harmonic system that predates equal temperament. Technical complexities like these may be evident aurally to first-time listeners, even if they don't know what the term means. Better not to worry about it: yield instead to the majesty and power of this grand contrapuntal study.

According to one commentator, the preludes and fugues of *The Well-Tempered Clavier* are Bach's only compositions in F-sharp major.[13] Certainly the key, with six sharps in its signature, is a product of equal temperament, rare in music before the nineteenth century. Later composers—Chopin, Mahler, Debussy, and Ravel, to name a few—used it often and with ease. Bach's prelude and fugue in F-sharp major in Book I are an exquisite pair. Bach conceived the prelude, a broken-chord study in dance rhythm, in two voices that intertwine beautifully to the ear without actually doing so on the keyboard. The melody that emerges from the figuration is tranquil, ineffably lovely, nearly ecstatic; the gently sway of the rhythmic web is one of Bach's most delicate. The three-part fugue opens with a lyrical subject, soon joined by a chiming countersubject in faster-moving notes. The countersubject's bustling joy seems to dominate the contrapuntal texture and mood to the end. It's all too easy for this marvelous pair, modestly proportioned but well matched in mood, length, and texture, to get elbowed aside by their deeper, darker, broader-shouldered companions, such as the F-sharp minor prelude and fugue that follow.

The F-sharp minor prelude and fugue call to mind the F minor pair we may recall from just before, where a choreographic prelude, technically instructive and light in texture, sets the stage for a fugue that is mammoth in scope and old fashioned in style. It may be that this prelude is a bit less rich in texture, yet more pungent harmonically than its F minor cousin, but their kinship is unmistakable. Much freer in construction than the F minor, this prelude opens in opens in two lean voices, the top one setting out a fluid, finely spun line above a mincing rhythm in the bass; but about halfway through Bach introduces a third voice, then a fourth, as his needs arise. But even in four voices, the composer manages to keep the textures light, probably by keeping the musical flow light and easy.

But the huge fugue in four voices is another matter, built on an ago-nized, old-fashioned, upward-creeping subject into which Bach builds a heart-stopping pause, and rounding it out with a powerful trill. Even David Ledbetter, who focuses on the technical and historical and tends to be reticent about the music's emotional content, notes, "In sensi-tive hands its pauses can be made to express an extraordinary depth of experience."[14] As Ledbetter also points out, this intense, deadly serious passage articulates a single, dark affect, which the drooping countersubject in faster notes serves only to intensify. It has been an overwhelming contrapuntal demonstration for nearly every composer, musician and listener who followed, of the devastating power of the fugue in the hands of its greatest master.

A wild pair in G major succeeds this somber essay. The prelude, short and fast, is in unmistakable toccata style, opening with scrambling triplets over a bounding figure in the bass. The hands alternate the material, then both play triplets, famous for their difficulty of execu-tion. The vitality of this prelude is immense; here we see Bach, almost godlike in his playfulness, dispatching his material in the grandest style, but doing so in only nineteen measures that take barely a minute to play—assuming you can play it! The fugue in three voices, a mag-nificent companion piece, sounds like a movement from a concerto by Vivaldi. Its subject is based on the common, four-note melodic device called a *turn*, set to a vigorous and powerful dance rhythm that seems to gain strength as the fugue progresses. Bach builds a structure of surpris-ing length and density from his simple-sounding, spinning theme. The writing is busy for both hands throughout, as the composer introduces trills and exciting quick notes to the texture. By the time he reaches the climactic moment of the fugue (bars 79 to 81), the counterpoint is so wound up that he needs a few comical measures to unravel the dizzy motion of the three voices.

Another exercise in melodic turns animates the G minor prelude. Rather like its siblings in F minor and F-sharp minor, this is a melodi-cally oriented, decorative piece, light in rhythm and texture, and not without charm. It opens with a trill that's a full measure long, which recurs three more times, making a stronger impression every time.

Here, the turns don't appear until almost halfway through, then dominate the piece to the end, which is itself a long sequence of turns, concluded by a trill, but this one short and ornamental. A subject with a strong profile, including a pause and a chromatic melodic step forms the dominant element of the four-voice G minor fugue, a powerful example, if not quite as long as some of the other fugues that are as serious in tone. But the affect here is obviously troubled and expressive of pain, in a manner the prelude lacks. A flowing countersubject offers some relief, but it doesn't enter until the fugue is three-quarters finished; in the last line, too, the second part of the subject rises up, as though perhaps trying to break free.

The wagging figuration that dominates prelude in A-flat major puts it in the style of a concerto or a chamber sonata. Certainly the brisk and cheerful opening statement might remind listeners of the Italian Concerto's first movement. And the way Bach passes the material from hand to hand is concerto-like. Finally, the busiest notes take over, dominating the movement, their momentum driving the thematic material to the end. The four-voice fugue sounds suave but is, to some, awkward in spots to play. The opening notes return, gloriously harmonized like chimes, at its conclusion.

The contrasting prelude and fugue in the rare key of G-sharp minor form an interesting pair in every way. The prelude, a long-limbed, lyrical conception of extraordinary grace, is based completely on the material set out in the opening bar, yet seems like a single, melancholy line or breath. Although Bach surely conceived it as a dance, it seems to anticipate the barcarolles of Chopin and Fauré, with their long, wave-like, melodic lines that intertwine, resulting in some gorgeous harmonic complexity—just as can be heard here, though Bach writes in just three voices. How those voices droop, rise, then droop again, always with the greatest elegance, makes this prelude one of the (relatively) little known marvels of *The Well-Tempered Clavier*.

The four-voice fugue, based on a menacing subject, based on a stepwise motion with stabbing repeated notes that make the tune stay in the memory. Bach works some ear-catching, jazzy rests into the entry of the fourth voice, and the incisive repeated notes dominate the counterpoint at the end. But there's a tight, tough, ungiving aspect to this fugue.

The prelude and fugue in A major form an interesting pair, with the prelude suggesting a gliding dance in impeccable three-part writing. The opening theme is one of Bach's most amiable, but of course he complicates everything in the middle of this short piece, introducing syncopations, dips into minor keys, and inversions of the thematic elements. Faster notes take over in the long closing phrase. There's no sense of hurry; rather, of an intensification of the contrapuntal process.

The subject of the three-voice fugue is one of the most striking in *The Well-Tempered Clavier*: a single note, followed by three beats of rest, then the remaining notes. Since it's played at a quick tempo, the rest is not long in duration, but it is so unusual as a thematic texture that, with it, Bach forcefully grabs the listener's attention. The subject is built on the interval of the fourth, unusual and tricky for this kind of exercise, manifesting itself in the chiming sound that dominates the counterpoint and harmony. The rhythm of the fugue gives it a strong choreographic feeling, and the notes break into a joyful gallop at several points.

The A minor prelude and fugue are dissimilar, the prelude a charming little study in concerto-like writing in a long graceful dance beat, the fugue—one of the longest in *The Well-Tempered Clavier*—an all-stops-out exercise in contrapuntal display and unmistakable affective fury. The prelude opens with a statement of its mincing theme, supported by a kind of slow trill in the left hand. Those who know the music of Vivaldi may hear that master's influence. The waters run deeper at center of this brief movement, as Bach thickens the harmony, working through a pulsing, anxious passage. The fugue subject is not unlike that of the G-sharp minor, with an angry, stabbing theme. This long four-voice fugue is difficult to bring off for many reasons, chiefly due to the repetitive nature of its rhythm; and a lack of variety between the episodes is also a problem. And overall it seems to lack the concision of fugues of comparable, or greater length—the C-sharp minor of Book I, for example. It seems wrong for mortals to criticize Bach, but the A minor fugue might be a rare example of the great composer's being just a bit off his game.

The B-flat major prelude opens is a quick and brilliant toccata-like movement. It opens with a capering broken-chord figure that breaks into scales, then more substantial chords stated in the sharp rhythm of a French overture. In the second half of this brief movement, Bach plays out the contrasts among these three elements—broken chords, scales, and full chords—throwing in an impressive trill for good measure. In the end, the broken chords scamper off, high on the keyboard, in a manner similar to the gigue that closes the B-flat major Partita. The three-voice fugue has a hopping subject reminiscent of the well-known two-part invention in F major. The composer makes much of the busy tail of the subject and a hammered five-note figure heard first early in the movement. Here the dance rhythm is strong and the affect joyous, though, of course, the bright surface is supported by complex contrapuntal art.

B-flat minor was another key unheard of in Bach's day; Chopin would use it often and to great effect. Somber but grand, the prelude and fugue in B-flat minor clearly had their effect on the Polish master. The prelude, unusually rich in texture and free in construction, is based on a theme in a short-short-long rhythm, obsessively repeated, and stated in harmony ripe with dissonance that's at once painful and gorgeous. An inner voice pulls insistently downward, itself a fine example of true keyboard writing, adding an almost intolerable gravity to the thematic flow. Later, Bach thins the texture, freeing the theme from the downward drag of lower tones, and indeed the music reaches higher for a while, but as he thickens the texture again, it seems as though the melodic flow is freezing over. Finally, Bach halts on a massive, dissonant chord, followed by a pause, then embarking on the closing sequence, which, with a sense of terrible inevitability, pulls the melodic material down once and for all.

In the fugue, one of the noblest conceptions in *The Well-Tempered Clavier,* the composer seems to have transcended the suffering-laden affect of the prelude. The subject, a grandiose idea on its own, is marked by two long notes, a rest, then a gigantic leap (of a ninth) followed by a steadier flow of quarter-notes. A rare example of a fugue in five voices, this majestic study employs the older style of counterpoint, making it sound like a church motet of a century or more before Bach wrote it, with entries of the subject coming in initially from the highest to the lowest. Filled with many arcane contrapuntal devices, the fugue will affect the first-time listener with its somber beauty and spiritual exaltation.

Another rare key for a baroque composer, B major elicits from Bach a lovely pair. The prelude is fairly straightforward, but some buzzy harmony gives a pastoral feeling. The melodic structure is similar to that of the opening movement of the Partita No. 1, with an ambling melodic figure unraveling above a rising accompaniment in the left, then the material passed between both hands. But that *praeludium* is more varied in texture as well as more elaborately ornamented, while this expresses an almost demure simplicity from start to finish. The four-part fugue, based on a long, confident theme unfolds in a radiant splendor at which the prelude hardly hints.

The great prelude and fugue in B minor that concludes Book I together form one of Bach's most daring creations. The prelude is a sonata movement in the baroque sense, like Scarlatti's, Corelli's, or Bach's own as heard in the chamber works, based on dance rhythm and consisting of two parts, both repeated, in which the second answers the first, like the allemandes in the dance suites.

In both prelude and fugue, Bach gives rare tempo indications, that of the prelude being *andante,* which means "moving along," a kind of easy walking speed, neither fast nor slow. But apart from the tempos, little about this music is easy. It opens with two voices in the right hand, moving in a slithering syncopation, above a rock-steady bass line in the left. There is a great deal of dissonance as the upper voices clash, at times with an almost metallic glitter. Yet the music is at the same time meltingly soft as the two upper lines come together, then separate. And it is extraordinarily beautiful. In the second half, Bach inverts the opening material, complicating it in every conceivable way. There is greater movement in the note patterns, and more complexity in the harmony, which was far from simple in the first half. The affect of this music is not easy to pin down. Many hear suffering, which is difficult to dispute. But there's also an eeriness; and a faint menace that pervades it, too. Finally, its tight rhythmic profile contrasts powerfully with, and sets the stage for, the broad subject of the fugue.

Nothing could be more remarkable than the alarming, chromatically conceived, and very modern-sounding subject of the enormous four-part fugue that ends Book I: Bach presents all twelve tones on the keyboard in its reptilian twenty-note length, ending on a long trill, unrolling in a steady, stately flow of even notes from which Bach has banished choreographic feeling and implications. The composer gives it a tempo indication: *largo* or "broad," a very slow tempo. This shattering melody contains all possibilities of suffering and grief, which Bach's stupendous development bears out: the glittering countersubject that coils and uncoils around it; the dissonances "of terrifying beauty";[15] and the heart-easing subject of the episodes, based on a little phrase in the prelude that passes most hearers unnoticed. The chromatic nature of the subject also gives the fugue a sighing and weeping affect absent only in the episodes, when the more comforting theme drawn from the prelude reigns. This towering contrapuntal essay shows Bach at the peak of his powers, in a sovereign display, giving the fugal process a cosmic power.

The Well-Tempered Clavier, *Book II*

ach seems to have begun compiling material for the second volume of *The Well-Tempered Clavier* right after finishing Book I. As before, he composed some new music and revised existing pieces. Also as before, the set originated as teaching tools for his advanced keyboard students. By 1742, when the composer was fifty-seven years old and in command of one of the most complete and profound compositional techniques in history, he completed Book II.

The quality of Bach's output over the course of his career is high and even, so it's impossible—and it would be foolish—to characterize or rate these immense collections: Books I and II are equals on their lofty plane, though the first volume seems to be the better known. Charles Rosen notes, "The second book . . . differs only in being generally a little more sober, more inward, less ostentatious, and, perhaps, less various as a whole."[1] There's a slight difference in style: Bach's writing more of Book II in the so-called *galant* manner, lighter in texture and more straightforward thematically than the old contrapuntal techniques. The high classical style of Haydn, Mozart, Beethoven, and Schubert, in which melodies reign over their accompaniments, descends from the *galant*. Bach wrote many of the Book II preludes in this new style, a preclassical sonata form in two sections, also employed by Scarlatti in his brilliant sonatas for keyboard. And, indeed, one might hear an overall textural lightening. Some are in the *stile antico*; many are in the dance-based style fashionable in the middle of the eighteenth century. A few fall into neither category but are hybrids, and compositional experiments. In any case, Book II of *The Well-Tempered Clavier,* contemporary for its era yet beyond time, contradicts the image of Bach as a musical reactionary, looking only backward.

The first prelude and fugue of the second book are magisterial. The opening movement, which Bach subjected to a number of revisions, is reminiscent of a prelude for organ, opening on a thunderous pedal point above which elaborate figuration unfolds. From this sea of notes the theme, of great breadth and Olympian in tone emerges, gradually but grandly. Bach subjects it to some intense alterations—thematic, rhythmic, and especially harmonic—before returning to the home key. At one point the texture is almost impenetrably thick, and the affect hard to discern. The eleventh prelude, in F major (CD Track 7), is built in a similar way. The three-voice fugue, based on a subject in a joyful dance rhythm, is also regal in tone.

The pair in C minor that follows is beautiful and interesting in many ways, notably for the contrasts the pieces present with the imperial prelude and fugue that precede it, and also for how greatly they differ from the C minor pieces in Book I. The prelude is a two-part sonata movement in the baroque sense, with two halves, both repeated. In this fine-boned piece the composer sets a quick, delicately pattering figure in one hand against slower notes in the other, though at some moments the hands work busily together. And the fugue, unlike its rollicking sibling in Book I, is a serious, four-voice affair in which Bach puts his dignified, unchoreographic subject through its paces, then adds some rather dramatic flourishes at the end.

Both the prelude and the fugue in C-sharp major are astonishing works, the prelude a murmuring takeoff of the famous broken-chord opening prelude in C major of Book I, here rendered in the most exotic of all keys, to which the composer then appends a passionate, dancing *fughetta*—a miniature fugue. The full fugue is a comic essay on a bumptious, ludicrously simple subject. The prelude opens like that of Book I, number one, with two broken chords to a measure. Here, though, Bach adds a third voice, in the form of a throbbing line in the middle; the affect remains tranquil, with the hazy tonality casting its peculiar shadow, but all the while that pulsing middle voice builds tension. Suddenly the composer stops, tosses at us an arching theme based on a turn, and lets it spin in the quick-time, seconds-long *fughetta* in three voices. The real fugue, also in three parts, opens with an almost silly subject that huffs and puffs over a few notes before opening out into an impressive comedy that perhaps foreshadows the masterful contrapuntal writing of Verdi's *Falstaff*. In Bach's fugue, shorter note values assume an ever-growing role, finally running away with the piece in the last few bars. This C-sharp major prelude and fugue are music of the highest sophistication.

As are the strongly contrasting paired works in C-sharp minor, with the prelude being one of the most beautiful in *The Well-Tempered Clavier*. A rising figure in a long, lilting rhythm sets the mood for this exquisite and lavishly ornamented slow movement in three parts. Different critics hear in it different inspirations. To Donald Francis Tovey, the great English musicologist, it's a "trio in the style of a great slow movement in a piece of chamber-music,"[2] which makes a great deal of sense. Landowska hears Bach's admiration and skilled mimicry of the dance pieces by French keyboard composers, "most of all by Couperin. . . . The prelude is crowded with ornaments of every kind. . . ."[3] Her recorded performance beautifully demonstrates her view. When one adds up what these experts say, it might be that Bach was inspired by more than just one of the many styles he had mastered, all of which he fused seamlessly into this sumptuous work.

Opinion varies about the three-voice fugue, too, a piece in dance rhythm that seems close in spirit to some of the driving, sometimes fierce gigues that conclude the French and English suites and the third, fourth, and fifth Partitas. The triple counterpoint is remarkably complex for a process that rushes by so quickly, and there are disturbing chromatic slips and slides, and an ending that's short, if not exactly abrupt. Different performers play it in very different ways: Tureck treats it like a rough, tarantella-inspired gigue, as does Jandó on his Naxos recording; but taking a contrarian's view, Landowska cautions against "treating it like a gigue. The mood of this Fugue is incontestably serious and demands a moderate tempo."[4] And of course, her recording offers a convincing display of her interpretive approach.

In Book II, Bach abandons the quirky humor of the D major prelude in Book I, to return to more standard affects and practice for this key signature. The opening movement is a vast overture-like piece in the triumphant mood he often reserves for this key. The opening theme, built on a figure that rushes up, then descends in a mighty swaying rhythm, is very much in the same mood as several of the composer's other D major excursions, including several choruses in the B minor Mass and the spine-tingling chorus "Jauchzet, frohlocket" that opens the *Christmas Oratorio,* radiant with trumpets and drums. Here the tone is nearly identical and the outline of comparable breadth, if of course without the splendor of chorus and orchestra. But this prelude is quite spectacular, too, and it's easy to imagine it orchestrated in the same brilliant way as its choral cousins. Composed relatively late in Bach's career, some modulations between keys anticipate the harmonic drama of the classical sonata, which began to develop around the same time.

The four-voice fugue, based on a serene, hymnlike subject with a strong profile of repeated notes, is another example of the composer deploying the *stile antico*—the Renaissance polyphonic style. Its affect is prayerful but confident, with none of the agonies of the old-fashioned fugues from Book I. This is also a breathtaking contrapuntal display, with stretti—entries of the subject—coming thick and fast. Bach achieves magnificent display of counterpoint with what sounds to mortal ears like frightening ease.

Bach fills the D minor slot in Book II with another tempestuous pair, much like those in the first collection. From the sharp turn in the left hand and downward-rushing scale in the right, he throws the listener into an atmosphere of demonic energy and excitement, with the clear influence of Vivaldi. The texture is light, like a two-part invention, but the impetus of the music is wild from beginning to end, almost as though about to spin out of the composer's hands—though of course it never does. The thematic elements and figuration jump from one busy hand to the other, as the piece seems to run down, then into an abrupt chord, where it must stop. The slithering subject of the three-part fugue opens with a sequence of swaying triplets, followed by a troubled, sighing chromatic fall in its second phrase. Despite its obvious beauties and relative brevity, this marvelous contrapuntal exercise is filled with Bach's profoundest technical magic. There is, for example, a great deal of syncopation to refresh the rhythmic patterns, and he uses the chromatic side of the theme to make many bold harmonic alterations.

A sweeping melody emerges from the dancelike figuration that opens the gorgeous, subtle E-flat major prelude. Some commentators have noted the similarity of this prelude with the opening of the Prelude, Fugue, and Allegro, also in E-flat, which the composer wrote in a quasi-plucked, lutelike style. That same sound, of widely spread broken chords, and quietly joyful mood are common to both works. In this stunning examples of his musical art and artifice, like the music for solo violin and cello, Bach makes us hear what notes suggest, sometimes by dancing around an implied tone, but never actually sounding it. The four-voice fugue, conceived in the Renaissance choral style, is filled with long-held notes and is calm and triumphant in tone, a hymn of praise. These pieces, dissimilar in tone and texture, make a fascinating pair that work well together precisely because of their differences.

The fine-boned prelude of the big D-sharp minor set that follows is as different as it could be from the massive chords and high-flown rhetoric of its opposite number in Book I. Here Bach gives us the steady flow of two equally weighted voices, in texture a two-part invention in all but name. This, however, has the two-sections form of a sonata, allemande-like in its motion and twisting intensity, the second part acting as both a reply to and intensification of the first: where a voice rises in the first half, it falls in the second, where Bach also elaborates thematic material in quicker notes. These, Landowska rightly asserts, "must not be rushed, but played with a clear and expressive touch."[5] A delicate melancholy, bordering on morbidity, also unites this movement with many of the dance suite allemandes.

The subject of the tremendous four-voice fugue that follows opens with repeated notes, like that of the D major fugue just discussed, but their affects differ in every imaginable way. Whereas the D major is calm and confident, this one paints the mature composer's tragic vision. The fugal texture is mostly thick, and Bach's expressive and sophisticated chromatic distortions give this grand lament an air neither antique nor modern, but instead timeless. And yet, except where Bach catches the subject in webs of syncopated rhythm, then agonized clusters of chords just before the end, his conception is fluid and poised, his art transcending—in a manner not unlike the B-flat minor fugue of Book I—the suffering it articulates.

A spacious study in touch is the technical matter the composer presents in the E major prelude. Written in three voices in sonata style, the movement has two halves, in which the second comments on and deepens the thought of the murmuring idea expounded in the first—none of which speaks to the divine beauty of this extraordinary prelude. Bach proportions the second half even more generously than the first, following the climactic passage in high notes by a long (fully ten measures of twenty-nine), exquisite closing phrase. The mammoth four-voice fugue is another exercise in the *stile antico,* a tribute to Palestrina, and, according to one critic, to Girolamo Frescobaldi, the superb composer of works for keyboard of a century before Bach, whom the later master admired and studied carefully.[6] One interesting aspect of this fugue is how the generic, rising-falling nature of its subject receives a stupendous working-out: a staggering stretto entry of the subject, sung out in pealing notes by the highest voice, leaves listeners dazzled, as though at the gate of Heaven. It's also the most vocally styled of all *The Well-Tempered Clavier* fugues, with that the four parts falling within singable range; it has been arranged for and sung by choirs.

The cool beauty of the E minor prelude comes from the delicacy of its two lines, which make it sound like a two-part invention; this, like the D-sharp minor and E major preludes we have just looked at, is also in late baroque sonata form, with two parts, both to be repeated. This one, marked by a frequent, long, buzzing trill, has a fantastical quality also reminiscent of the Fantasia movement that opens the A minor Partita. Yet in spite of its textural delicacy, this dancelike movement is neither small, simple, or short, running about four and a half minutes when played with repeats. The subject of the long but fast three-voice fugue that follows is notable for its swagger—or snarl—derived from the turns in the second bar, as well as from the inflection marks Bach gives the notes, indicating that they should be detached, and finally from a sequence of hammered triplets. All contribute to the forceful, even aggressive character of the fugue, which shows the composer's intimidating side. He halts the fury of the counterpoint about two-thirds of the way through, leaps back into the fugue, then ends on a bold, toccata-like passage, where one voice resumes what seemed to have unwound, as Bach changes tempo from the brisk pace of the fugue for an adagio recitative of a few notes, and then back to tempo for the concluding phrase—strong stuff.

A twilit majesty pervades the sublime F major prelude (CD Track 7), in which the composer conjures thematic material and solid chords from sweeping figuration built of scales and broken chords. His harmony is rich and forward-looking, including all kinds of pulls toward F minor and other keys, but the affect is one of unsullied serenity. It's more important to take in the vast scale and ecstatic tone of the prelude than to worry about the techniques Bach uses to achieve them. Although the music may be complex technically, a few landmarks are worth listening for. Note, of course, the sweep and tidal grandeur of the main theme, then at 0:06, listen for the A-flat, which pulls the harmony toward the minor, adding only richness with no sense of a "sad" affect. The dusty sound throughout the prelude comes from Bach's astonishing freedom, both with keys and with notes that don't belong to the key he's in at a given moment. The main theme reappears in different keys at 0:38 and 1:15, in slightly varied form at 1:08 and 1:53, and finally in its original form at 2:11. Listen to the flowing notes that melt together into a big chord, starting at 1:46, in perhaps the clearest example of the prelude's dominant texture. And in the most harmonically daring episode in the movement, listen to the passage starting at 2:00, where Bach cuts boldly across tonalities as he prepares the reprise of the main theme.

The fugue in three voices, based on a cheeky subject in an incisive gigue beat, is as different as could be from the broad soundscapes of the prelude. As in the E minor fugue, Bach indicates detached notes, here giving the melody a scampering quality. Also in this track, the first voice enters at 2:54, the second at 2:58, and the third and lowest at 3:07. A scrambling phrase in the right hand at 3:40 foreshadows a tendency that becomes more pronounced and funny as the fugue progresses, finally bursting out in a wild sequence from 4:27 to 4:32. There's also a good example starting at 3:57 of a pedal point, where the bottom voice sits on a single, deep note for more than four bars before resuming its busy activity again at 4:03. That Bach realizes this happy contrapuntal dance with the utmost sophistication should come as no surprise.

Hypnotic and enchanting, the F minor prelude is based on a pathos-laden, weeping motif set out in a steady, ticking rhythm. The texture is straightforward for Bach, with the three voices scrupulously respected but little contrapuntal friction between them. The broken chords, however, are interwoven into the thematic material with admirable artfulness. Formally the piece is in the late baroque, preclassical two-part sonata, like Scarlatti's or C. P. E. Bach's, just coming into fashion as the old style—J. S. Bach's own polyphonic style—was passing. The fugue, based on a vigorous subject in the rhythm of a bourrée, is a witty exercise in a more simple style of fugue-writing and an exploration of the harmonic implications of the diminished seventh, an expressive interval that was one of J. S. Bach's favorites.

The F-sharp major prelude and fugue possess strength and lightness, the prelude offering some elements with rhythmic profile similar to the French overture, the rhythmic stiffness of that form undercut by the steady flowing stream of notes underneath. But the composer's marvelously inventive web is also delicate, staying in two voices almost throughout, adding voices for a bit of additional weight only in the last three bars. Its many trills and grace notes anticipate the trill that kicks off the fugue, another dance-based essay, like the preceding three, in E minor, F major, and F minor. This one has for its subject an elegant gavotte, whose witty, equally urbane countersubject in repeated notes appears about a quarter of the way in and chugs imperturbably alongside the subject. Though they go by quickly, this pair is quite substantial in length and content; Bach's management of them is deft.

The F-sharp minor prelude and fugue is, without question, one of the greatest in *The Well-Tempered Clavier,* drawing the most flattering comparisons from critics. Tovey, for example, compared the breadth and flexibility of Bach's phrases in the prelude to Milton's,[7] as though the composer needed flattering comparisons with great poets. Cooler and more apposite, Ledbetter hears in it the influence of Bach's own work, notably the Fourth Partita's vast allemande. In any case, the opening sequence is another extraordinary sinfonia, a splendid compositional and technical exercise in three voices. Notable for the gentle but insistent tug of its syncopations, and, indeed, the rhythmic variety of its thematic articulation, this glorious movement is a profound form of expression. What its affect is, precisely, seems harder to name; some hear tenderness, others grief.

The fugue, a tremendous exercise in the old polyphonic style, has three subjects: the first, a tragic, sculpted phrase clothed in a stern rhythm concluding with a trill; the second a falling companion of a firm, masculine character; and the third, a steady, murmuring figure in sixteenth notes that acts as background until the end, highlighting the powerful personalities of the first two. This is a titanic work that meditates deeply and darkly; though, as it often does, Bach's music seems to break through the pain it depicts.

The G major prelude and fugue make a joyous pair. The free contrapuntal style of the prelude sets two voices against each other; a third, in long-held notes, comes and goes as Bach needs it. The hands trade the thematic material, which consists of a two-against-one pattern in a chase that never sounds like mere display. That is the role of the short, brilliant fugue in three parts, based on a burbling dancelike subject. A series of comical scales, reminiscent of the Partita No. 5, also in G major, round out this fugue that is short in playing time but remarkable for its force and wit.

The big G minor prelude and fugue stand in stark contrast to the previous pair. The main theme of the prelude, a kind of French overture, is stated at the beginning in stern dotted notes, its tempo, largo, given by the composer. The tone is dark and troubled, but the grandeur of Bach's expression gives the music a luscious richness. A shift at the very end to G major acts only to emphasize the depth of the darkness through which the modulation cuts. The fugue, based on a memorable subject in which a stabbing repeated note is prominent, may remind some listeners of the G-sharp minor and A minor fugues in Book I in its vehemence, though here Bach's polyphonic treatment generally seems smoother. But his forcefulness stays intact, particularly in the dramatic, even savage pauses that mark the closing passages.

The prelude in A-flat major is one of the longest Book II and one of the grandest, as well. It opens with a billowing chord sequence set above a rhythmic pattern clearly inspired by the French overture style, setting for it a figurative context. But this bold and beautiful piece can in no way be heard as a French overture; rather, it's a free and original form developed by Bach for this piece, drawn from his immense knowledge of musical techniques and styles. The big chords are trailed by single notes in floating figuration, which then give way to a texture that's predominantly in two parts. Bach mixes and develops his ideas and textures freely and with absolute assurance, and his harmonies here are wide ranging and daring. Many hear in the prelude's stately rhythmic patterns a kinship with the mighty Sanctus chorus from the composer's Mass in B Minor; indeed, they do resemble each other, sharing a spacious grandeur.

The four-voice fugue that accompanies this glorious prelude is based on a subject that exudes joy. A countersubject in running notes adds intensity and rhythmic excitement. Bach builds to a big climax, followed by a coda—a closing passage—in which subject and countersubject unravel excitedly.

In addition to possessing a hypnotic charm and beauty, the G-sharp minor prelude is interesting from a historical standpoint: it's one of the most advanced in style in *The Well-Tempered Clavier,* a study in the homophonic early classical manner of which his son, Carl Philipp Emanuel is perhaps the greatest exponent. What we hear is a melodic structure that dominates a steady accompaniment in flowing notes. Bach's own style placed equal parts into polyphonic play; and even here the accompanying figure is more independent minded than most in the classical style. Bach actually returns to a stricter form of two-part writing over much of the course of the movement. But the dominant tune, a running figure ending in a striking sigh, is unmistakable. This marvelous music has a delicious, melancholy lilt.

The double (two-subject) fugue in three voices that follows is as one might expect a serious essay in polyphonic writing, yet like the prelude it, too, has a graceful air. This comes from the sweeping lilt of its 6/8 beat. The two subjects are, first, a long, looping, and pretty one, then a falling one with strong chromatic inflections, which deepens the tone with its strong downward pull. Bach cast this forward-looking movement, remarkable, too, for its chaste and sober grace, in a style that combines his contrapuntal mastery with the lighter *galant* textures in fashion in the mid-eighteenth century.

A doubled version—12/8—of the rocking rhythm of the previous fugue turns the A major prelude into what baroque composers (and later ones, as well) called a *pastorale*. This category indicates a gentle and lyrical music, in the style of this wonderful piece. Bach employed the flowing 6/8, 9/8, and 12/8 time signatures often in his oratorios and cantatas to indicate Christ and his birth; those who have heard the famous chorus "Jesu, Joy of Man's Desiring" from Cantata No. 147 or its transcription for piano will recognize here the same serene joy. Bach's technical artillery in achieving a calm, pleasing affect is of course formidable: as the piece progresses, he extends the melodic span, which is already long, and also inverts it. The composer also throws in some gorgeous complications of the harmony. The brisk three-part fugue is based on a rising subject, which leads to a rattling development, notable for Bach's deployment of a figure in an exciting, dotted rhythm.

The A minor prelude, an allemande-like study in two parts, is based on sinking chromatic melodic lines, in a compositional feat that seems to extend those lines beyond what is possible. Both hands' material seems only to fall, though of course it does occasionally rise, to start at once another drooping phrase. In the second half of the movement, Bach inverts the themes; if you imagine his standing them on their head and changing their movement, you'll get an idea of what he is doing. But the chromatic nature of the voices—their characteristic sliding sound, as opposed to stepwise melodic motion—makes their trickle uphill at least as laborious and painful as the downward movement of the first half. Although chromatic writing inevitably lends a somber tone, sometimes the motion of the mincing, exceedingly dainty twin lines here may serve a comic purpose. One critic at least[8] hears satire in the outlandishly emphatic statement of the subject of the three-voice fugue, four spat-out long notes, followed by seven in quicker time, spinning into a tail of very fast notes and trills. The over-the-top vehemence of this fugue has few parallels in the composer's keyboard output, making it an outlier, even in the oeuvre of an artist used to expressing himself freely.

Bach sets the long-limbed and beautiful B-flat major prelude in a rapturous dance rhythm. The theme combines triplets and a bouncing element into an exquisite texture in which the composer moves freely between two voices and three, and asks the player to cross hands, a technical challenge that's easier on a two-manual harpsichord than on a piano. The two sections of this sonata movement are fully in the fashionable *galant* style of the mid-eighteenth century. Here Bach develops his theme, though not in the conflict-laden manner of the high classical era; in the second part of the movement he digs deeper, finding new aspects of his material, which is, after all, pretty rich. The fugue, based on a long subject of gently hammered even notes, very unusually marked by Bach with slurs, indicating he wants some of them connected, which adds a sighing quality to their sound. Although only in three voices, the counterpoint is dense, as Bach works in two additional subjects. Yet what probably strikes many listeners is the fugue's suavity.

Vast in scope, the B-flat minor prelude and fugue stand among the grandest in *The Well-Tempered Clavier*. The passionately expressive prelude seems to burst with sorrowful affect, which, typically, the composer reins in—though just barely here. And the enormous four-voice fugue, built on a potent subject that opens with long notes interspersed with pregnant rests, then more flowing notes, is a titanic creation, Michelangelo-esque in its density and force, a sublime moment. Bach delivers its searing emotions via his loftiest technique, pulling out all the technical stops, but he sublimates everything to the grand scheme, pacing his episodes to give balance and moments of relaxation to his immense polyphonic fresco. Is this the last fugue in *The Well-Tempered Clavier* in the *stile antico*? Perhaps—but it's also an example of art that is timeless, transcending considerations of style to speak with infinite force and eloquence.

A marvelous showpiece for the keyboard, the B major prelude is also of radiant good cheer. It opens with glittering scales, which give way to a bubbling passagework; midway through the work a charming melody, draped in grace notes; it emerges over a lively left-hand accompaniment. The scales and more brilliant passagework over a comically bouncing bass notes returns; the piece ends on a rich passage, farther down the keyboard—in deeper notes—than the listener might expect. The four-voice double fugue is big boned but radiant, its character completely different from that of the prelude. The theme suggests that its working out will be in the old-fashioned style, but Bach takes a more modern approach instead. The first subject rises, falls, then rises again in steady, even notes, and the affect is serious and deeply joyful. Bach drapes the second subject, in flowing notes, lovingly over the first, and at the end he brings to prominence a little phrase from earlier in the work. A shrewd dramatist, he throws nothing away.

Bach forgoes immensity in the B minor prelude and fugue that conclude Book II, so those expecting or hoping he might try to top the gigantic Book I pair in the same key will be disappointed. The syncopations common to both preludes are the only common element; the Book II prelude is an unusual and interesting piece based on the turn, the four-note spin that animates several other preludes. Even though the composer moves his melodic building block all over the keyboard, it sounds vocal, like singing. This is a quirky piece that reaches a rather heated climax, then spins itself out in urgent, broken phrases. The wonderful three-part fugue is a bouncy passepied, a dance found in abundance in the English and French Suites and the partitas. This fugue, rich in wit and choreographic grace—its minor key notwithstanding—makes a brilliant, low-key stage exit from the grandeurs and rigors of the Book II preludes and fugues. Bach knew exactly what he was doing.

Dance Suites II
The Partitas

Bach composed seven works in the partita category: six between 1726 and 1731, when he published the group as the first volume of his *Clavier-Übung* ("clavier practice"). The third and sixth, in different versions, had already appeared in the Anna Magdalena Notebook of the early 1720s. The seventh partita, less known but every bit as magnificent as its companions, is the French Overture in B minor, published in 1735 as an element in the second volume under the same neutral name, made up of two of Bach's finest and most exciting keyboard works, the other being the Italian Concerto. In common usage, as Bach employs it here, these partitas differ structurally and stylistically hardly at all from a suite, like their predecessors, the so-called English and French.

But in these later works the composer displays a greater structural focus, and in some more ambition. Some of the English Suites, notably the sixth and last, may be longer in playing time, but the Partitas seem more tightly organized and concentrated in expression. The first six also offer an artful and carefully calculated progression in size and intensity, opening with an urbane and charming work and ending with a one vast in dimension and unmistakably tragic in import. In between, the composer alternates works lighter in tone and texture—but in no way slighter artistically—with more ambitious, heavier suites. The first, third, and fifth fall into the first group, whereas the second, fourth, and sixth are larger in scale and denser in their keyboard writing. Composed later, the French Overture stands on its own level of expressive complexity, opening with the longest movement of all, but ending with a series of light, fantastical *galanteries* unlike most of those in the prior six.

In the six Partitas published first, Bach seems to try to cover all bases, titling each opening movement differently, these being *praeludium, sinfonia, fantasia, ouverture, praembulum,* and *toccata,* respectively. But three of the seven—the second, fourth, and unsurprisingly the seventh—begin with substantial overtures in the French manner. Five conclude with gigues (the second is the exception, ending with a capriccio), of radically differing characters. Allemandes, courantes, and sarabandes come as standard equipment, but *galanterie* movements inside the suites also speak to the composer's desire to show his ability to command a variety of dance rhythms and styles. The second Partita—of Bach's works one of the most French in style—has a *rondeau.* The third, a singular suite without an ancestor or descendant in the composer's oeuvre, a *burlesca* and a scherzo. The immense fourth may appear closest in form to the English and French Suites, but is bigger than the latter, more tightly structured than the former, and again, different from both types in its character. It has as extra movements an aria and a *menuet.* The short but radiant fifth has a *tempo di minuetta* and a passepied. The *galanteries* of the tremendous, tragic sixth are an air and a *tempo di gavotta*—a fierce gavotte. The independent-minded French Overture stands alone in having no allemande, but offers instead an embarrassment of riches in the way of *galanteries*, with two gavottes, two passepieds, two bourrées, and, following the gigue, a singular, extraordinary movement entitled *echo.*

Bach is at his most polished and elegant in the exquisite Partita No. 1, in B-flat major. In this deservedly popular suite, the composer seems to have purged all rough edges from his style, offering music where everything, from parody to rustic references, is achieved with complete artfulness and assurance. The first movement, entitled *praeludium,* opens with a delicate melody that widens like an opening blossom from its initial B-flats and trills, reaching upward. The composer passes it from hand to hand, introducing some longer runs into the picture; held notes also contribute to its ever-thickening textures. Themes reappear regularly in inverted forms or in the other hand from the one that first played them. The movement concludes with a passage harmonized to display the strong side of the main melody, something we may not have perceived in it in its earlier, gentler guises. Deeply lyrical yet highly organized, this beautiful movement is a pure keyboard conception.

The allemande opens, like the first movement, with a repeated note pattern that quickly breaks into a melody that flows out of streaming arpeggios. The passage that concludes the first half is rhythmically complex, richly harmonized, and difficult to play. The second half, as anyone familiar with the form now knows, is more dense harmonically, and with a whiff of sublimity that is unmistakable as Bach guides it infallibly to the home key. Even though gossamer textures make the music sound as though made of air, it is, of course, woven of a material that is light but tough. A strong skipping figure in the left hand dominates the courante, here given is Italian name *corrente,* which also presents its melody initially in repeated notes that then expand their range quickly. Most of the right-hand part wreaths the tune in triplets, the familiar rhythmic device that packs three notes into the space of two, giving it a throbbing, or as here, a bounding quality. Some of the jumps assigned to the left hand are wide and difficult.

A feeling of improvisation pervades the sarabande that opens with a phrase built on notes and chords, which are repeated thoughtfully and then expand outward. The second half begins by mirroring the first, then moving further afield harmonically, giving to the left an expressive, cellolike passage under a long trill in the right. The feeling at the end is a satisfying sense of coming home. Two of Bach's most charming minuets serve as *galanteries.* The first is an smooth imitation of a rustic instrumental duet, with sawing figuration in the right, and detached notes in the left achieving the effect with delicacy and no rough humor, except—perhaps—for a scurrying figure in which the right hand, in parody of the fiddle, rushes to catch up. But there is really nothing rustic about this little dance. The tiny second minuet, only sixteen bars long, sounds like celestial chimes.

The closing gigue stands alone among Bach's dances in this genre for several reasons: first, it's in a straight, two-beat rhythm unusual for the form; also, there are hand crossings in every measure. Apart from the brilliant keyboard music of Domenico Scarlatti, which Bach may or may not have known, this showy technique was unheard of in 1726. In any case this gigue, built of a melody and accompaniment recombined into arpeggiated triplets dashes with Chaplin-esque grace through its rainbow of harmonies, particularly varied and dazzling in the second half, without losing its balance. Toward the end the tune and accompaniment fall and rise chromatically, then scamper off in the upper reaches of the keyboard, rather than finishing on conventionally stated chords; Bach accomplishes all this with breathtaking elegance, spirit, and wit. This great movement, light in tone and texture yet with the tensile strength of a spider's web, forms a perfect conclusion to this wonderful suite, itself a testament to the ability of music to display character, strength, and substance while remaining quick on its feet.

One look at the score of the Partita No. 2 in C minor tells another story. Bach's tempo marking, *grave*—"slow and solemn," modified only slightly by the next word, *adagio,* "at ease," suggests a gravity quite different from the buoyant delicacy of the previous work. Indeed, the opening passage, built of massive chords interspersed with a regal figure in what is known as a *dotted* (long-short) rhythm, re-creates the proud atmosphere of a French overture with a correctness that would do any native composer proud. Like this one, most French overtures consist of an opening section in a stately dotted rhythm, followed by but connected with a quick, dancelike movement, generally enriched contrapuntally. As in the French Overture—the seventh partita—in partitas there may be a reprise of the opening passage, but there is none here. Bach loved this form, using it fairly often, and always to great effect. Other essays for the keyboard in the French overture style include, as noted, the opening movements of the fourth and seventh Partitas, and the D major fugue in Book I of *The Well-Tempered Clavier.* The brilliant sixteenth *Goldberg* (see page 120) is also in the form.

But the dramatic gesture that opens the second Partita is that and only that—dramatic affect. This is no stage tragedy but a lively and brilliant work in which the composer displays his love of French musical style. A long melody, slow but incisive, and strongly suggestive of the plangent tones of the oboe, follows the brief but weighty opening passage. The melodies of this section and that of the opening movement of the French Suite No. 2, also in C minor, are close cousins. The roulades surrounding it grow more lavish and complex as the passage proceeds, ending finally in a trill that feels like a pitcher's wind up into the fast, contrapuntal part. Here the expression moves from the songfulness of the long oboelike section to the urgent dance rhythms and rich fugal textures of the closing portion of this overture in three parts. Its dashing theme seems to leap boldly ahead; soon it's joined by a second voice in an exhilarating, choreographic fugue that recalls several of Bach's others in the same key and mood. Although longer than the ornamented passage, it moves much more rapidly, ending on a dramatic cadence that recalls the opening phrases without quoting them. Professionals say that it is far from easy to play.

Some of the open feeling of the B-flat Partita returns in the allemande, built on a gracefully descending theme that seems nearly weightless. Yet complexities soon intrude, as they always do in Bach's allemandes. In this case they include some harmonic diversions and a pull into the deeper region of the keyboard. As usual, the second portion is graver and denser in harmony and texture, reflecting a deeper abstraction. An exceptionally fine and rhythmically complex courante, based on a long, arching melody, follows. Bach ornaments the theme copiously, in a very French manner, then in the second half subjects it to inversions that make it twist, turn, and stand on its head with a more Germanic intricacy.

A theme similar to that of the courante in its curving profile opens the very beautiful sarabande. This is also one of the most flowing movements of its type in Bach's keyboard works, built on steadily moving arpeggios instead of solid chords, like many of his sarabandes. The melody of the *rondeau* that follows is marked by a big downward jump and infectious skipping rhythm that brands it instantly into the mind and memory. Like all pieces in rondo form, this one alternates the main theme with complementary episodes. And to make his own job more interesting, Bach varies the theme on each of its three recurrences. This is a forceful movement, with a strong profile that nevertheless maintains a delicate texture.

And the wonderful capriccio with which the composer ends the suite in place of the normal gigue is another brilliant binary dance that's notorious among performers for its difficulty. Here, "Bach amuses himself royally,"[1] in Landowska's splendid phrase, taking his sharp-edged, exciting theme and moving it briskly from hand to hand, inverting it in three-part keyboard writing that takes great skill and control to keep untangled. Note when you listen to the theme its appearances at the opening, then in the left hand, and again in the right. Listen, too, to the great, jumping bass figure that plays so important a role in the movement, but which actually appears first as part of the main theme in the right hand. Bach inverts his material in the second half, bringing the music to a great, rollicking high point. Here, again, the minor key does not remotely suggest a "sad" affect.

The Partita No. 3 in A minor is the quirkiest of this series by a long way. Although its textures are light, like those of the first and fifth Partitas, its mood is troubled—though not consistently. This work is one of two Partitas, the other being the big No. 6, that appeared in slightly different forms in the Anna Magdalena Notebook. Some critics perceive inconsistencies of tone and dimension among the movements, particularly the light-footed sarabande and the big, grim gigue.[2] But a particular wiriness of texture and taut construction that distinguish this suite are evident in the first movement, a fantasia that sounds like a two-part invention. The quick 3/8 beat resembles that of a passepied, but the inward tone and knotty part-writing are like none of Bach's other dances of that name, which tend toward a lighter elegance. But the clean and clear weaving of the two voices that compose this wonderful movement offer much that is beautiful and very characteristic of the composer. When well played it sparkles, while never giving up its characteristic dark tone.

The allemande that follows is heavily ornamented, the short notes giving the music the illusion of moving faster than the moderate pace usual for this dance. A fevered atmosphere sets this allemande apart, as well. The courante—here given by the composer its Italian title of *corrente*—is a fierce affair with a sharp rhythmic contour. Although Bach keeps its texture light, the forward motion has all the considerable bite he can summon. In the second part, he inverts and expands the material.

The sarabande is one of the composer's most unusual, a dainty version, unlike any other, with a light texture and strong forward momentum. Here are no sequences of chords in exalted or tragic tone; rather, a delicate and fine-boned dance that is difficult to compare to anything in Bach's oeuvre. The two *galanteries*, a *burlesca* and a scherzo, also stand as singular if slender landmarks in the composer's output. The first is another edgy two-part dance that seems to struggle to contain dark emotion beneath its surface. And the scherzo also bites, with small but sharp teeth. Do not look in its ninety-second length for anticipations of Beethoven's massive symphonic scherzos, or of Chopin's dramatic masterworks of the same name; there are none. The gigue that ends the work is the biggest movement by any standpoint, recalling those of the English and bigger French Suites. Its urgency and denser keyboard writing place it in another class from the other movements of this curious suite, all of which do at least share a certain delicacy of texture, if not of tone.

Superlatives are in order for the Partita No. 4 in D major, the longest and grandest of these suites. Here, every movement is cut on an heroic scale, and the music radiates a glorious light and heat that puts it in its own class within Bach's works for keyboard. Yet for all its outward splendor, the musical content is profound, too, with every movement of the highest quality, and an allemande and a sarabande that both achieve sublimity.

Bach's makes his high ambition obvious from the start. The first movement, entitled *Ouverture* (CD Track 8), is a fully developed French overture, opening with a stately sequence in full sonority and regal dotted rhythm, followed by a long fugal passage in a beautiful, swaying dance beat. Even the first chord, magnificently spread across the keyboard and containing within itself a splendid trill (0:01), sounds spectacular, demonstrating the composer's lofty purpose. A rushing scale in the left hand follows, by a figure in dotted rhythm, all features of the French overture. More important than the minutiae of stylistic conventions, though, is to attend to how well Bach has captured its proud and pomp-laden spirit, maintaining its genuine grandeur. The dotted figure, interspersed with scales that bustle stiffly up and down the keyboard, form the meat of the opening section. Trills and grace notes, freely interspersed, are also part of the style, as are the bracing three-note figures, first heard at 0:27 but which dominate the texture from 0:41 to the end of this section.

At 1:20 the opening passage is repeated; at its conclusion, the fugue theme, which seems to drift downward with an easy, choreographic lilt, enters (2:33). The second voice of this three-part fugue enters at 2:38, and the third at 2:50; but again, it's more important to enjoy the wavelike beauty of the rhythm and lightness of feeling than to worry about the counterpoint, which is confident and clear. But be sure to enjoy the playful sequences at 3:43 and 5:10, and the minor-key ones that dominate the middle of the fugue, starting around 3:52. At 5:45, Bach begins to thicken the textures, as he moves toward the climactic passage at 6:10 and on to the end.

In his thoughtful study *J. S. Bach: A Life in Music*, Peter Williams notes that the composer seems to have a systematic purpose for using the form of this movement, halfway through the six Partitas that make up volume I of the *Clavier-Übung:* "A central overture is like the 'inner exordium' of a sermon, the moment when the preacher 'starts again' for rhetorical effect."[3] Williams is correct: all the second halves of the four volumes of the *Clavier-Übung* open with movements in the dotted rhythm of the French overture. In all of these, Bach finds the power of the French overture, and the sureness with which it arrests an audience's attention, the means to restate his ideas and to restart his sets midway through.

The allemande that follows is one of the most beautiful and profound Bach ever wrote; it also may be the longest. Pianist Wolfgang Rübsam takes almost twelve minutes to play it (on Naxos records, from which the selections on this book's CD have been drawn), taking the repeats of both halves, meaning that he plays everything twice. Glenn Gould's 1957 performance, in which no repeats are taken, runs 6:27, showing consistent timing between the two: the movement is exceptionally long for its type. The reason why is because Bach doubles its proportions, with each half of the dance consists of twenty-four measures instead of the more normal twelve, like the slender one from the B minor French Suite. The result is a movement that the listener perceives as expansive and unhurried, as though the composer is breathing (and thinking) more deeply. Its melody is long, articulate, and fervent, deeply meditative in character. Bach ornaments it generously from the start, and adding more decoration and rhythmic shifts as it progresses, bringing to its joy a more passionate mode of expression that manages to hold a profound calm as well. The effect of this dance is much like and entirely comparable to what a great slow movement would have in an instrumental composition from the classical or romantic era; but in this vast work, there's room for two, the second being the sarabande.

The courante, also a sizable specimen, is built on a splendid, curling theme with a ceremonious quality absent from most of these. As in the allemande, Bach finds way of expanding the form. Here he writes in a broader beat than usual and gives the left had a more flowing accompaniment. The melody is swathed in ornamentation as it rises and falls. The aria that follows is, like the other airs and arias in the dance suites, a jaunty, incisive binary dance with a memorable melody. Yet even this little movement seems broader in dimension than comparable *galanteries* in the context of this large-scale work.

A descending phrase like a celestial sigh opens the great sarabande, as noted the longest in the Partitas, in which Bach returns to the ruminative yet exalted tone of the allemande. The opening phrase stops, as is in wonderment, on a long-held high note before gently resuming motion. From the opening Bach drapes his lovely, halting melody in ornaments that grow more lavish and intense in expression as the movement proceeds. Like its sibling movement in the C minor Partita, this sarabande is built chiefly of flowing melody and relatively straightforward accompaniment, rather than chords (which Bach breaks into arpeggios when they do appear), making it more songful, and more like a true dance, as well—but giving it sublime beauty. As in the allemande, the composer stays tightly organized while moving at a leisurely pace; it is best when listening to let go of distractions for the few minutes it takes to listen, and let Bach take the lead.

The melody of the minuet is spiked with triplets, giving to the dance a more pressing feeling than its sweet-natured melody might otherwise provide. Triplets also dominate the texture of the spectacular gigue (CD Track 9) that ends the suite. Listen to the whiplash of the loopy opening phrase, and note how it immediately opens out. Contrapuntal entries come in quickly, at 0:08 and 0:18, and the second half of the dance begins at 1:52. But Bach never lets flag the driving momentum of this astonishing combination of gigue, tarantella, and fugue. Most remarkable is the lightness of touch with which the composer executes his many tasks, which include not only writing an interesting fugal gigue, but of providing an aesthetically satisfying ending to this large-scaled, seven-movement work. He needed to find the right tone for his final movement after the grandeur of the opening movement, and the depths plumbed in the allemande and sarabande. These he accomplishes with the assurance only the greatest artists possess, with the joyous speed and brilliance of this movement that never touches ground. Inevitable but miraculous, this virtuoso tour de force seems the only possible ending for the fourth Partita.

With the opening notes of the Partita No. 5 in G major, the composer brings us firmly back to earth. The *praeambulum* is a toccata-like movement where comedy and lyricism mix freely. But the opening gesture of an intentionally banal falling scale followed by the simplest of gravity-laden, flop-down chord sequences; then a longer scale, followed by the same chords, displays a remarkably earthy humor. There are more plain scales, these going up; some arpeggios; then another downward scale and dumb chords. A light-footed, lyrical melody emerges from busy figuration, then widens gorgeously: more arpeggios, scales, and chords. And so it goes in this taut and brilliant movement with material alternating drolly. Comedy makes an unmistakable appearance in the chortling thirds in the left hand, but the lyrical theme turns out to be as powerful in its way as the comic bits, and seems to win out in the end. What is interesting here is the sonata-like way Bach treats his ideas, presenting them initially in starkest contrast, pitting then against each other, before combining them deftly. Lyricism dominates the allemande as well, which develops a theme of great beauty, elegantly draped in billowing triplets and trills. The *corrente* (the Italian drive of which inspires Bach to give the title in that language) is a bristling, bustling, airborne version of this quick dance that so often displays a hard edge.

Rather like that of the Partita No. 3, the sarabande here is unusual, this one displaying a rhythm resembling that of a minuet, and employing a more delicate texture than normal, too. Bach also decorates it generously. The diaphanous *tempo di minuetta* may be the most charming movement in all the Partitas, its textures so fragile as hardly to be there. Its melody soars, though, and the composer uses a rhythmic device (with the medical condition–like name of *hemiola,* for those keeping track) that broadens the way the floating melody is phrased and adds a pleasing ambiguity to the rhythm, making more irresistible what already seemed delightful; and the passepied that follows is also very appealing. Again as in the third Partita, Bach ends the suite with a gigue of greater weight, dimension and difficulty than what has gone before. But whereas the gigue of the A minor Partita is all scowling intensity, this is a jolly fugal dance, showing the composer at his most magisterial. The inversion of the theme in the second half seems to show Bach in that mood of easy and playful mastery when showing off and having fun at it. Although shorter and lighter in keyboard texture than the two huge works that flank it, the Partita No. 5 is magnificently conceived and executed. Throughout, Bach holds confidently to his chosen wiry keyboard style and lyrical-comic point of view that is singular within these suites.

In the Partita No. 6 in E minor, we see Bach at his most troubled— and troubling. Although just as ambitious and almost as long as the glorious fourth, the sixth espouses in comparably lofty style a far darker point of view. This, as noted is one of the two Partitas that appeared in an earlier version in the Anna Magdalena Notebook.

The Partita opens with a toccata, large in proportions and power, cast in three clearly delineated sections. The immense, almost tactile opening gesture consists of an arpeggio that reaches up to a dissonant chord, sculptural in its grandeur. A series of rushing scales, are followed by a long phrase in which two notes in the left hand grind painfully against one in the right follow, then light chords echoing the sharp dotted rhythm of the opening. The first section consists of alternations and reiterations of this gripping material, ending at last on a grumbling phrase in the left, the subject of the grim fugue in three voices that forms the central panel of the movement. The constricted range of the subject and the narrow portion of the keyboard to which Bach keeps it combine to make this section claustrophobic; despite some sequences in major keys, its tone is unrelentingly gloomy. The composer weaves the grinding passage from the opening section into his contrapuntal fabric as a countersubject, which finally pulls the fugue back inexorably to the terrible opening figure, as the third section of the movement begins. Here Bach sticks to the arpeggios, dissonant chords, and scales, omitting the grinding phrase that dominated two-thirds of the toccata, as the music seems to withdraw gradually from view, ending on the light, taut chord sequence. (In his 1957 recording of the work, Glenn Gould pulls back in volume for the closing chords, giving the phrase a devastating remoteness.)

Gloom persists in the allemande, transformed by the composer to a delicate melancholy that borders on morbid. Its falling, heavily ornamented theme, set out in a dainty mincing rhythm defines the brooding abstractedness of the tune. The closing cadence spells out the tonic chord in a way that sounds obsessive yet dreamy. Unusually, the second section is two bars longer than the first; usually they match exactly. Bach does this by stretching the second half of the theme into a longer, heavily decorated and still more sorrowful meditation. The closing phrase again breaks the closing chord, tracing it into a moody arpeggio.

The extraordinary *corrente* is the longest in the Partitas, with two themes. Its textures are light, but Bach captures a surprising range of emotions, including the pain of the opening toccata and the morbid gloom of the allemande, and adds to it a profound unease as well as the barely veiled menace this dance often displays. The unquiet comes from the syncopation of the first theme, stretched uncomfortably over the steady, stabbing bass, and providing much of the music's nightmarish quality. But the silvery runs that dominate the right hand take the morbidity first set forth in the allemande to a new plane. Complementary with the movements that precede and follow it, this dark dance shows how carefully the composer arranged these movements into a coherent whole, even though some of his material was older. He liked this movement a great deal, recycling it in slightly different form for a version of the Sonata in G major for Violin and Harpsichord.

The air is the lightest movement in the work, a rushing, spirited affair that grants a moment's rest to the careful listener's by now perturbed spirit. The sarabande, however, goes right back to the broodings of the allemande, and by dint of the most extravagant decoration turns the solemn theme into an intimate and detailed confession in tone. As usual, the second half is more intense than the first, and the ornamentation even wilder. The *tempo di gavotta* returns to the sharp tone of the *corrente,* but is more straightforward rhythmically and seems to have its feet planted firmly on the ground. But it, too, has an undeniable menace.

With the closing gigue, Bach returns to the titanic scope and the terrors of the opening movement, here set forth in a fearful stamping rhythm and a harmonic scheme dominated by endless, jarring sevenths, an expressive dissonant interval the composer loved dearly. Sevenths can easily be made to sound beautiful, but here his presentation of them is so tough and relentless that conventional beauty is one of the last impressions a listener will come away with. This grand but comfortless dance leaves us no doubt about the tragic stature of the work it concludes, one of the masterworks of the keyboard literature.

The French Overture in B minor, published in 1735, is the second of the two works that compose volume 2 of the *Clavier-Übung.* The first piece is the Italian Concerto; in paring the two Bach demonstrated his mastery of the national styles he admired. Both stand among the high points of his maturity, with the full richness of his imagination and complexity on full display. Originally in C minor, Bach transposed the work to B minor, a more exotic sounding key that most keyboard players also find less comfortable than the original tonality. There is some speculation as to why he did this, but no certainty. Another interesting characteristic of the work is that Bach omits the allemande movement, a crucial element of his conception in all the other keyboard suites, whether the French, the English, and the first six Partitas, balancing the grandiose opening movement with seven *galanteries*—far more than any other contains. Adored by those who know it, this extraordinary suite is inexplicably and absurdly less popular than the first six Partitas.

The first movement, a three-part French overture, opens with a statement in dotted rhythm of the theme, magnificently imperious. Like the Partita No. 4, a long, fast, fugal passage in a swaying dance rhythm follows. But this one, in a tighter time signature, pushes ahead aggressively, whereas its D major sibling, moves with a longer limbed grace. This section is also notable for its alternation of passages in close succession marked by the composer to be played *piano* (soft) and *forte* (loud). Here Bach, who composed the work for a two-manual harpsichord, desired a dramatic effect, one that is unfortunately less effective on a modern piano. (It makes sense to listen to performances on both instruments.) At the end, he returns majestically to the opening passage, which he restates in all its potency and splendor. The score calls for the player then to repeat the entire fugal section and the reprise of the opening; although it may be lovely to hear everything again, the magnificence and dramatic force of the return of the opening passage is compromised.

One of the composer's more eccentric courantes follows, intricate and convoluted in the right hand, but with some repeated notes, atypical for Bach—though very French sounding—in the left. The first *galanterie* movements, a pair of mincing gavottes, follows. The second stays in a very narrow range of the keyboard, played much more easily on a two-manual harpsichord than a piano. Two passepieds follow, the first a great, driving one, the second a gorgeously ornamented centerpiece in the contrasting major. In both *galanterie* dances, Bach instructs that the first one played again after the second, formally satisfying to the listener's ear and helping as well to fill out this already substantial suite. Like those in the C minor and E minor Partitas, the sarabande is of the flowing rather than the more static, chordal type. It is also intensely chromatic, meaning that Bach throws in additional notes that give the music a shifting, slippery sound that anticipates some of Schumann's early piano works in its unpredictable harmonic wanderings, and in the density of its keyboard textures, too.

Two splendid, driving bourrées follow, sharp, aggressive, even jazzy, then a gigue in a light, skipping rhythm that recalls those of the French Suites.

For good measure, Bach throws in the spectacular *echo* to end the work. The term refers to the rapid alternating *pianoforte* effect he spells out carefully in the score, before the final, rollicking statement of the tune under a triumphant accompaniment. Little before the twentieth century matches this incredible short dance for the its memorable theme, yet even more for its boundless drive, set to a jump rhythm that leaps across two centuries in an anticipation of jazz, shocking in its force, joyfulness, and clarity.

The Individual Works
Singular and Significant

W hen we think of Bach's works for keyboard, those in organized series tend to dominate our view: six partitas, published together (of course, with the French Overture, added later), six French and English suites, and the forty-eight preludes and fugues of *The Well-Tempered Clavier,* where twice in his career the composer explored the twenty-four keys. We humbly presume he employed sets like these because they allowed him to display his command of a wide range of forms, styles, and technical difficulties of all kinds. Also, it was a common practice to publish musical compositions in groups of six. But Bach also wrote many individual works, several of which stand among his best and most popular.

Among Bach's most important and interesting individual pieces is the *Capriccio on the Departure of the Beloved Brother,* which is also one of the composer's earliest-known compositions. Composed when he was about twenty, the *Capriccio* is an important early landmark, possessing immense youthful charm and energy, clearly foreshadowing the glories of Bach's mature style, as well.

Its title has undergone what Christoph Wolff describes as "a widespread but inauthentic adjustment"[1] from . . . *the Beloved Brother* to . . . *His Beloved Brother.* The error arose due to the proximity in time of the departure to Poland of a Bach brother, Johann Jacob, to the composition of the work, inspiring editors and publishers to a bit of wishful biographical speculation. Wolff and other serious scholars doubt the connection of the music with the event. Nevertheless, as he notes, scores and recordings are far more likely to carry the incorrect title.

Capriccio means "caprice," suggesting a fantasy-like work that's light in tone. Parts of this *Capriccio* unquestionably fit the bill, whereas others wear a more serious affect that never seems other than a mask, which the composer picks up, then drops easily over the course of its six brief and lovely movements.

In structure the work is a descendant of the *Biblical Sonatas* of Johann Kuhnau, naive and charming suites for the keyboard that illustrate Biblical tales in music. Other important composers, including Frescobaldi and Froberger, also preceded Bach in writing important descriptive music for the keyboard. Bach's work shares with Kuhnau's considerable charm but seems far more studied and refined. Whereas Kuhnau illustrates the Bible, Bach works from a more mundane scenario: someone is leaving on a long journey, uncomfortable and dangerous. At the head of each little movement is a verbal description of what the music depicts. In the first section, the would-be traveler's friends plead with him not to leave. In the second, they luridly describe "the casualties that could befall him abroad"; the third is a lament by his friends. "Here the friends come, seeing after all that it cannot be otherwise, and bid farewell," is the subject of the fourth section. Moving away from narrative, the fifth imitates the coachman's horn call; and the purely musical sixth, a rousing fugue based on a horn call–like subject, has no dramatic program but provides an artful and satisfying rounding out of the work.

The opening section also carries a musical title, *arioso,* which has several meanings, mostly relating to vocal music; Bach uses it here to tell the player that he is to employ a cantabile style, meaning that it should have a singing quality. The music does sing, or at least speak in a convincing imitation of human communication. The composer sets forth a repetitive rhythm, mostly in a rising notes laden with trills and turns that really can be heard as voices, pleading "please, don't go!" The second section, laden with bold harmonic shifts, is speechlike, too, voices clashing painfully as they list the dreadful risks of the trip. The third section is a lament, based on an old-fashioned drooping theme in the left hand (a ground bass, just as in Dido's lament in Purcell's *Dido and Aeneas,* or Bach's own *Goldberg Variations* of forty years later) followed by eleven tiny, exquisite variations, also fraught with expressive dissonance. Here the variation structure seems to dominate the descriptive content of friends lamenting the departure.

In cheerful voices drawn by Bach in big, bold chords, they rally for the next section—all of eleven bars that take half a minute to play—to bid him a convincing instrumental image of a manly good-bye. In the fifth movement, also brief but charming, the composer paints in tone the approach of the coach that will take the main character away, using the sonic metaphor of the coachman's stirring horn call. In an artful final gesture, Bach writes a not small, three-part fugue on a subject into which the most prominent phrase of the previous movement is woven.

There are worse ways to spend twelve minutes than in listening to the *Capriccio on the Departure of the Beloved Brother*; one can relish its directness in comparison to the complexity of Bach's later work, or use it as a blueprint to find many of the tracks on which his musical style would run. And it provides a marvelous insight into the passionate, humorous, energetic nature of the young master.

The mighty Chromatic Fantasy and Fugue apparently had a long gestation period, with early versions going back to the composer's time in Weimar, from 1714 to 1717, and reaching its final form around 1730. A creation of musical sophistication, passion, and power, this has always been one of the most revered of Bach's keyboard works.

As the title suggests, the work is cast in two large sections, a big fantasy followed by a fugue of comparable dimensions. The term *chromatic* refers to the notes in between those of standard harmony; the black keys, if you will. Composers well before Bach's time—Gesualdo, Monteverdi, and Frescobaldi, for instance—found in them a way to describe in music the pains of the flesh, and their unmistakable sighing sound always imparts to music an unmoored, anxious feeling. Bach uses chromaticism from the beginning of the *Fantasy* to the end, according to experts,[2] in a strictly conceived progression typical of his structured approach. But the feeling of the piece is of the greatest freedom, even wildness. The affect of the *Fantasy* is fearfully dark, perhaps too dark to name; Martin Geck speculates that Bach turned an idea he'd worked on earlier into a heaven-storming lament for his first wife, who died in 1720. And while the *Fantasy* has a toccata's rapid motion and difficulty, with lots of fast notes and changes of pace, it seems in a class of its own, well beyond Bach's works of that name.

A blazing scale that rises, falls and rises again, a stark pause, then another scale open the work, followed by broken chords and more scales. Eventually this pattern gives way to tremendous arpeggios, interrupted by an articulate, recitative-like phrase, then more arpeggios. These majestic broken chords strongly resemble those for violin in the contemporaneous Chaconne for solo violin, also in D minor— and equally titanic. A passionate, operatically styled passage marked *recitativo* follows, then broken phrases alternating with scales, as Bach steers the music deftly through a sequence of astonishing harmonic modulations. This bold passage shows the composer's skill at moving effortlessly from one key to another, and is another piece of evidence that he used equal temperament tuning. (See the discussion of temperament and tuning on pages 56–57.) Scales take over again, interspersed with recitatives, as the piece winds down to a conclusion that's quiet but extraordinarily dark.

Once heard, the sliding fugue subject is impossible to forget. The rage and passion of the music seem to storm against the structure of the three-part counterpoint. Booming notes in the bass foreshadow the music of the romantic movement; indeed, this work highly influenced many composers who followed. At the fugue's furious end, Bach recalls the opening of the *Fantasy* with a spinning scale, concluding this gigantic conception with a cyclical effect, ending it as it began.

The beloved Italian Concerto of 1735 is the sunny companion of the French Overture, the two works forming the contents of the second volume of Bach's four-volume *Clavier-Übung*. The former work, of course, shows Bach's mastery of the complex, densely ornamented French keyboard style. The concerto is the composer's tribute to the instrumental form made popular by such Italian composers as Corelli and Vivaldi. Bach loved this form; lighter, broader, and frankly melodious, it was conquered radiantly in this glorious composition.

Listeners used to thinking of concertos as having orchestras as well as soloists may be puzzled by the title of this three-movement work for solo keyboard. There are several reasons for the name. First, Bach viewed the concerto as more a style alternating denser and lighter passages, than as a strict form, and it was one he felt perfectly comfortable about adapting to his own needs as a teacher and performer. Also, since people who played the harpsichord at home were unlikely to have an orchestra to play concertos with, he simply adapted the style to a single instrument and player for home use. As we shall see, it's one of a number of concertos for solo instrument he created or re-created—they're more than mere transcriptions—from the work of other composers.

The second reason for the title is that Bach wrote the Italian Concerto for a two-manual harpsichord, the resources of which were on his mind and in his hands as he composed. With the instrument he could indulge in difficult passages close together, much easier for a player to cover when there are two keyboards. Also, the mechanical and tonal resources of the harpsichord allow the skilled player to clarify the contrasts between the passages representing the soloist and those that portray the imaginary orchestra. These, Bach delineates carefully throughout the work, characterizing the "solo" part by a single line, or sometimes two (he's not as strict here as when writing a fugue), usually fast moving, and the tutti—the "orchestral" part—with chunky chords. Finally, for tone color, Bach indicates contrasts in dynamics—loud and soft—as much as in any of his work, to imitate the Italian style, thereby giving the piece the vibrancy of a concerto performance.

The melodic force and rhythmic swagger of the unforgettable opening phrase (CD Track 10) display Bach's grasp of the Italian concerto: it sounds as though Vivaldi wrote it. Indeed, Bach admired Vivaldi greatly, but as the movement goes on we hear a harmonic density and flexibility that could only be Bach's. The opening phrase is followed by busy figuration in the right hand, above a dancelike figure in the left, beginning at 0:10; the busy passagework here, as through most of the Italian Concerto, represents the idealized solo part (for example at 0:36), be it an imaginary flute, violin, or harpsichord. The interplay continues over the course of the movement, through a sizable minor-key episode (from 1:11 to 2:00) and a series of witty trills for the "soloist" at 2:10, 2:15, 2:36, and 2:38. And to the end, this brilliant music is impelled by a relentless, dancelike drive. It also displays, alongside its worldliness and sophistication, a continual tonal magnificence and a radiant spirit.

In the slow movement (CD Track 11), Bach again captures the solo against tutti dichotomy with fantastic clarity. The rocking opening phrase for the left hand, which continues hypnotically through the entire movement, convincingly mimics the sound of the small baroque orchestra, over which the right spins an endless, passionate and melancholy melodic line, beginning at 0:16. Bach breaks the "solo" rhythm often with sobbing syncopations from 0:31 to 0:34, 1:57 to 2:00, 2:51 to 2:56, and 3:02 to 3:06. He also subjects this glorious melody to almost constant distortion with deeply expressive ornamental twists and turns. In the end, the "solo" and "orchestra" parts end together on an exquisite dying fall (4:22 to the end).

The finale (CD Track 12), given by Bach the tempo indication of *presto*—quickly—is pure glory, the upward rush of the joyous opening phrase a breathtaking musical tide. The melody is memorable, like those of the first two movements, and the momentum is greater than both, an outpouring of blazing energy. Bach's part-writing is dense and more difficult here as the thematic strands dance together and vie for dominance. As in the opening movement, there's a long, flowing passage in minor keys, from 1:32 until 2:46, and constant stream of furious passagework for the "solo" instrument or instruments. But again and again the up-rushing scale of the opening melody sweeps away everything in its path, and the movement ends in breathless triumph.

The Italian Concerto is not Bach's only concerto work for solo keyboard. There are also nine transcriptions of Vivaldi works: six for harpsichord, three for organ. These are infrequently played but delightful, as well as instructive on one of Bach's methods of digesting the Italian concerto style: he metabolized the works and their style by transcribing them. And all are very effective for their respective instruments. A hearing of Wanda Landowska's spectacular recording of Bach's transcription for harpsichord of the Vivaldi Concerto in D major will speak for itself: she gives Bach's loving tribute to Vivaldi its due. What you'll hear is the magnificence of Vivaldi's original, Bach's respect of its qualities—notably the dazzling energy—and his skill in capturing them. Finally, Landowska puts her virtuosity at the disposal of this brilliant takeoff. It may be out of fear of comparison with Landowska that harpsichordists rarely perform or record the Vivaldi-Bach transcriptions.

The transcriptions for organ are also great fun to listen to, even if they lack the harpsichord's incisive timbre, which seems to copy Vivaldi's sharp-edged, string-based sound more accurately than the organ can. But every dancing note is there, and then some: Bach could not resist enriching the works harmonically.

Bach engaged in another kind of transcription, as well: from one instrument to another. The Prelude, Fugue, and Allegro in E-flat major, composed around 1744, written perhaps for the lute, or more likely for an extinct keyboard instrument called the *lautenwerk*—the lute-harpsichord, which had gut strings, like the lute, for which Bach also composed another, more modest dance suite in E minor among other works. Today this piece is performed on the lute, harpsichord, or piano; its delicate textures seem to take least well to the modern instrument. There is an excellent performance by Elizabeth Farr (on Naxos) on a hypothetical reconstruction of a *lautenwerk*. The tone of the instrument is leathery but pleasant, and the recording is well worth hearing. And in any case, the composition is a magnificent conception on a grand scale that bears some resemblance to the E-flat major preludes of both volumes *of The Well-Tempered Clavier.*

This glorious work opens with a booming note in the bass, above which the right hand spins a hazy figuration, ecstatic in mood and in a broad dance rhythm. But the texture is fairly light, mostly in two expressive parts. The composer summons a third, briefly and delicately, toward the end. The texture and rhythm are reminiscent of that of the E-flat major prelude in Book II of *The Well-Tempered Clavier*, where figuration also floats above lutelike deeper notes that sound as though plucked.

After a short, meaningful pause, the old-fashioned four-part fugue begins modestly but builds to a huge, stretto-laden climax. This is one of the composer's instrumental fugues conceived in the *stile antico*—the Renaissance polyphonic style. After the climactic passage mentioned above, the music moves to a new central section within the fugue, an extraordinary murmuring passage of great beauty. Then, after the ruminations of this meditation, the fugue theme reenters, now entwined with the murmuring figuration. Finally, Bach resumes the fugue within, above, and around the material of the second part.

So densely does he weave and vary the thematic material that all melt together as one to the ear. But ultimately, the fugal texture takes over entirely. Thus, as Landowska (whose recording of the work is also highly recommended) observed, the three parts of this middle section form a triptych within the broader three-part structure of the work. It's also very reminiscent of the E-flat major prelude from Book I of *The Well-Tempered Clavier,* in which two sections, different in texture and structure—and one of them a fugue—are presented, then combined sublimely in a third incarnation that throws both into a new light.

The final allegro provides an earthy but brilliant last word after the celestial mutterings of the first two movements. A kind of two-part invention, it scurries along in long, dancing phrases, the upper voice playing two notes to one in the bass. This is fantastical music that moves with an immense energy that may sound muted to the novice listener, but only because Bach keeps to the two quiet voices. These seem to mix, quarrel, then find amity in the most calm, witty, good-humored, and elegant conclusion imaginable, a flawless musical version of a suave stage exit.

It would be an exaggeration to call the Prelude, Fugue and Allegro neglected, but it seems less frequently heard than its excellence merits—look for it.

As noted, these are not Bach's only one-off works for the keyboard. Two significant pieces that fall just below those described here in popularity and exposure are the Fantasia and Fugue in A minor (BWV 904), and a stray Prelude in Fugue (BWV 894) in the same key. The stormy Fantasia in C minor (BWV 906) is an impressive work that really is neglected in live performance but has at least been well recorded. Another rarely heard but fine set is the gorgeous, sweeping Prelude (BWV 923) paired with a long fugue (BWV 951) on a theme by the Italian composer Tomaso Albinoni, both in B minor. A D minor transcription for keyboard (BWV 964) of the Sonata in A minor for solo violin lacks the force of the original conception, perhaps because it sounds easier played by two hands on a keyboard, but is also very enjoyable.

Variations

Mostly the *Goldbergs*

Much about Bach's *Goldberg Variations,* the composer's grandest and best-known work in the form, appears paradoxical: the momentum and fantastical nature of the music rest on but contrast with layers of rigorous compositional structures; also, despite its length and complexity, the work stands among the composer's most popular, with 151 recordings of it available on the Arkivmusic.com Web site: a staggering number. This is perhaps understandable in view of the predominantly, though hardly exclusively, joyful character of the music.

A greater irony may be that although Bach evidently found the variation form uncongenial, he wrote what is universally acknowledged as one of the two greatest sets, as well as the more popular of the pair. The other member of this minuscule but illustrious club is Beethoven's *Diabelli Variations*; inspired by the *Goldbergs* and every bit as grand, yet less well known outside the music-consuming community. (Arkivmusic offers sixty-two performances of them, still impressive for a work of its length and sophistication.) The two works share a relatively upbeat point of view: the *Diabelli* standing, along with Symphony No. 8, among Beethoven's comic masterworks.

Musical variations take a clear-cut theme and then embroider or elaborate it. Most variations focus on the melody of the theme, but others, including Bach's few mature masterpieces in the form, use the bass—the bottom strand of the theme—to build upon. And never content merely to add grace notes or runs, drop predictably into a minor key, or shift the rhythm a bit, Bach squeezes every drop of harmonic power and expressivity out of his material.

Intervals—A Crib Sheet

The nine canons that form one of the key structural elements of the *Goldberg Variations* are described with a number: unison, second, third, fourth, and so on. What do these numerical designations mean? The simple answer is: they are *intervals,* the distances between notes. These apply to the *Goldbergs* in that each canon is based on a different interval, starting with the unison, then with ever-widening intervals, up to the ninth. What this means is that the second voice—the second thematic line of the canon—comes in at the distance of the named interval, each of which has a characteristic sound quality, and each posing for Bach a particular compositional test.

If you picture—or better yet, look at—a keyboard, you'll see that the black keys are placed in two groups totaling five; the first, of two, the second, of three. The note to the left of the first black key in the group of two is C, which we will use as our example. (For simplicity and clarity, we'll mostly ignore the black keys and the intervals they represent.) The white note to its right, D, is a second; the white key two to its right, E, a third; the third white key to the right (you've got it—F!) a fourth; next moving right is G —the fifth, A is the sixth; B is the seventh. The next note, also a C, is the octave, eight white keys away, and the next D, the interval of the ninth. Intervals that sound comfortable to the ear are called *consonant;* those that present an aural clash are *dissonant;* those that fit into neither category are *perfect.*

- The *unison,* which is the exact same note, presents no conflict to the ear, but makes it hard for the composer to differentiate the thematic lines in a canon.
- The *second* is a dissonant interval, meaning it presents a clash to the ear.
- The *third* is a consonant interval that sounds sweet and comfortable.
- The *fourth* and the *fifth* are perfect intervals, sharing an eerie, hollow sound that makes them troubling to the ear in extended passages and consequently tricky to compose in.
- The *sixth* is a consonant, sweet-sounding interval. One reason why will be clear if you count left from the next C you're approaching, from which it's a nice, consonant third down.

> ▪ The *seventh* is a dissonant interval, but highly expressive and much loved by Bach—and most composers.
>
> ▪ The *eighth*, or octave—the next C up the keyboard—is *perfect*, as you may expect, not painful to the ear, but it also sounds empty and is not easy to make beautiful. Finally,
>
> ▪ The *ninth*, a big, gaping interval from C to the D in the next octave up, is dissonant: the ear wants to hear it resolved.
>
> In theory, intervals continue on indefinitely, though all related intervals—such as seconds (C to the adjoining D) and ninths (C to the D in the next octave), thirds and sixths, and fourths and fifths—have a family resemblance. Also, keep in mind that every note—every key on the keyboard—has a structure of intervals built on it, just like the C we've looked at here. Since the *Goldberg* canons all use G as their basic note, the intervals there are all counted from G.

Bach's dislike for the melodic type of variation set can be inferred from his small production in the form. There is an early "Air with Variations in the Italian Manner," a beautiful, heavily ornamented work that seems to look backward as well as abroad in its keyboard writing, in its elegance and complexity reminiscent of the French school as much as the Italian. The intensity of its lyricism also seems to reflect the influence of the great English school of composers for the keyboard. Little heard, the work is well worth seeking out.

The Chaconne for solo violin and the Passacaglia in C minor for organ (CD Track 17) are, with the *Goldbergs*, immense exceptions to the rule of Bach's dislike; but these three titanic pieces share the structural similarity of being built on what is known as a "ground bass," a line that winds through the bottom of the theme, like the foundation of a building, which Bach repeats strictly or freely in every variation as a unifying structural device. Both works also are harmonic variations in that the composer uses themes built more of chords than of melody, which he then varies with greatest freedom, wielding the richest harmonic vocabulary of any composer of the age. The Chaconne and Passacaglia are, however, stately works, with dramatic and tragic points of view, far removed from the riotous, choreographic bliss of most of the thirty movements that make up the *Goldberg Variations*. The cataclysm Bach conjures from one violin working out the implications of the steely eight-bar chordal theme over a ground bass of the Chaconne demonstrates, like no other work, the incredible force of free harmonic variations on a ground bass. But of course an imagination like Bach's is needed to give it wings.

Bach's chief unhappiness with the variation form, according to Johann Nicolaus Forkel, his earliest biographer, was "the constant sameness of the fundamental harmony, [which] he had hitherto considered an ungrateful task."[1] This may be understood to mean that he found the variation form tiresome to work in because it was not adequately challenging or interesting, like counterpoint. As we shall see, in the *Goldbergs,* Bach creates then triumphantly solves his own challenge. He did so by writing "an immense passacaglia,"[2] rather than a set of conventional variations. So let's add one more irony to the list: the *Goldberg Variations* are "variations" only in the broadest sense of the word.

The *Goldberg Variations—Aria mit Veränderungen für Cembalo mit 2 Manualen,* Air and Variations for harpsichord with two keyboards, in its German title—came relatively late in Bach's life. It was published in 1741 as the fourth and last volume of the *Clavier-Übung,* the "keyboard practice" series that contains so many of his finest works for keyboard and organ. The tale of its composition will be familiar to anyone who has browsed the liner notes of a copy of any and all of those hundred and a half recordings, here related, then promptly debunked by Christoph Wolff, one of the most authoritative and reliable Bach scholars:

> Forkel relates the anecdote that the work came into being at the request of Hermann Carl von Keyserlingk in Dresden, who "once said to Bach that he should like to have some clavier pieces for [his house harpsichordist Johann Gottlieb] Goldberg, which should be of such a soft and somewhat lively character that he might be a little cheered up by them in his sleepless nights." However, all internal and external clues (lack of any formal dedication to Keyserlingk as required by eighteenth century protocol, and Goldberg's tender age of fourteen) indicate that the so-called *Goldberg Variations* did not originate as an independently

commissioned work but were from the outset integrated into the
overall concept of the *Clavier-Übung* series, to which they consti-
tute a grandiose finale.[3]

Now, two more paradoxes can be added to our lengthening list: that
the *Goldberg Variations* seem to be named for someone who had nothing
to do with them; yet the incorrect name is permanently attached and
far more concise, memorable, and colorful than *Aria mit Veränderungen
für Cembalo mit 2 Manualen.*

On paper, the structure of the *Goldberg*s is imposing. The work is
framed at the beginning and the end by its beautiful theme. Every third
of the thirty variations is a canon, beginning with the third variation,
with the interval of each canon widening as the work progresses. Thus,
the first canonic variation, number 3, is at the unison with the main
tone of the canon, whereas variation 6 is a canon at the second, and
so on, through to variation 27, which is a canon at the ninth. But with
variation 30 Bach breaks his pattern, writing a pastiche, known a *quodlibet*, of two popular melodies, both of which relate to the basic theme.
(Beethoven similarly found the structure of "Notte e giorno faticar"
from Mozart's *Don Giovanni* in Diabelli's little waltz, reinterpreting it
as variation 22 of his series.) Variations 4 through 27 fall into regular
groups of three, with the first, a character piece in a wide variety of
styles and moods; the second, a virtuosic toccata, mostly wild in temperament and all difficult to play; and the third, of course, a canon. But
Bach does not begin immediately with these—variations 1 and 2, serv-
ing as a gateway into the work, are written in the manner of two- and
three-part inventions. Similarly, as the work approaches its end, Bach
breaks the pattern with variations 28 and 29, brilliant toccata-like studies that are, respectively, mystical and comical in mood and expression.

All but three of the variations are in the same key (G major) as the
theme; these are variations 15 (the canon at the fifth), 21 (the canon
at the seventh), and 25, the great character piece that is the longest of
the variations by far and for most listeners the very soul of the work.
These are all in G minor. There is a break in mood at the center of
the work, following variation 15, the first in the minor mode, which
is followed by the overture-like No. 16 as the brilliant opening of the

work's second half. Bach varies his rhythm from one variation to the next. There are several variations (10, the second half of 16, 18, and 22) that are decked out in full contrapuntal style. Finally, if you are not sufficiently intimidated by all these audible patterns, scholars have discerned others—some numerological, others theological, and not all verifiable—that cannot even be heard, which Bach apparently wove in for his own amusement and to praise his God. It was always Bach's way to find his greatest freedom in the discipline of structure.

The theme of the *Goldberg Variations* (CD Track 13) is called by Bach an *aria*. Perhaps obviously, it is not an operatic one; the word here meaning simply "air," an old-fashioned usage for melody. This melody is a sarabande, a slow dance in 3/4 time in his Anna Magdalena Notebook. This wonderful melody—fervent, touching, and "already elaborately embellished"[4]—is played by the right hand, and is easily remembered. But the left hand quietly covers the notes—the ground bass—that form the work's real spine. The theme is in two sections of sixteen measures each; these are broken into eight-bar phrases that also divide with absolute evenness into subunits of four and two bars. Even though this may sound rigid, the theme is beautifully shaped, as harpsichordist Wanda Landowska wrote, "grave and yet happy, tranquil and at the same time vibrating with inner life. "[5]

So appealing is the right-hand melody and so rich are it its decorations, that it may be difficult for first-time listeners—or even those who know it well—to pay attention to the left hand, as well. But this is what you should try to do, without worrying too much about it—you can always replay it. Remember, in any case, that it is the left hand, playing the lower notes, that carry this complex, brilliant, and profound composition from start to finish. No doubt part of the composer's strategy was to conceal the true theme in the left hand beneath the exquisite, lavishly ornamented melody in the right. His purpose was to create a work (like the Passacaglia for organ and the Chaconne for violin) based on a harmonic variation and progression, allowing for a richer development than one based on melody.

The melody opens with right and left hands widely separated, creating a sound that is rich yet open. The first four-bar phrase, which lasts from the opening through 0:14, consists of two smaller units, the first at the very beginning; and the second, completing the first in lower notes, at 0:07. As noted, the melodic line is at once fervent and lavish, but listen, too, to the gently falling long notes in the bass at the start of each bar (0:01, 0:04, 0:07, and 0:11). Bach animates and enriches the left-hand part, as well, as you can immediately hear, but he allocates to the right hand most of the embellishment.

The second phrase begins (0:15) with an iteration of the same melodic pattern in the right hand, with the second half (0:21), the right hand bursts into gentle activity, echoed more tranquilly in the left (0:24). The third (0:29 through 0:42) and fourth phrases (0:43 through 0:58) follow a similar pattern, with the right hand embroidering the melody, with the left seeming to follow, moving at an easier pace. But the left's activity quiets once more in the final phrase (0:43, 0:46, 0:50, and 0:53). It's worth noticing, too, that the opening half of the theme ends in a questioning, hovering way. This is a pattern of melody and harmony that is structurally symmetrical and typical for themes used in the variation form, the second half completing the opening thoughts and seeming to answer the questions they pose.

From 0:59 through 1:58, pianist Jenö Jandó repeats the opening section, as indicated in the score. Not all performers play the repeats; this major interpretive decision will be examined later.

The second half of the theme beginning at 1:59, continues the delicate mood of the opening page, the change to the relative minor key of E minor adding poignancy. The melody reaches up to at beautiful turn (2:09), then pulls downward, modulating inevitably toward the closing phrase, which starts at 2:28. At 2:35, Bach increases the motion, with both hands moving at a steady pace, two notes in the right for each one in the left, where, again, the key bass notes are half-hidden. The melody reaches upward to a climax at 2:47, then falls into a graceful closing phrase. Again, Jandó follows Bach's instructions, repeating the second half of the theme (2:55 to the end.) This exquisitely sculpted theme, delicate but filled with emotion, offers a memorable and nontheatrical sequence of tension and release that Bach will exploit throughout the work.

The first three variations, as noted, form a pathway into the set. But they do not follow the pattern of character piece, toccata, and canon. Instead, the first variation is basically in the form of a two-part invention, in which a vigorous dance rhythm passes from hand to hand; there is some merry scrambling in the second half. Some performers, including Glenn Gould and Jenö Jandó, take this variation at a fierce clip; others, such as Landowska, move at a broader pace that seems more welcoming, but both interpretations work. The second variation, in three voices, moves more genially in tight counterpoint. The third variation, the first canon, is at the unison, a difficult compositional task, because the canonic imitation is hard to make audible. Yet this graceful piece moves in an easy, swaying rhythm over a dancing bass line. Bach provides all of the canons save one—the last, at the ninth—with a separate line in the bass. He instructs performers to play all three of the first variations on one manual of the harpsichord, providing a sense of containment, and making the canon more difficult to play than it would be on two, where the close writing might be split apart. Wonderful as these three pieces are, they only hint at the journey on which Bach will take us.

With the second trio of variations, Bach embarks on the structure that dominates the work. Variation four is a short character piece in a chunky rhythm reminiscent of a rustic dance. Its four voices crowd together, and Bach exposes the ground bass theme to more daylight than in any of the first three variations. The first written for two keyboards, the fifth variation sets the tone for all its toccata siblings that follow. There is busy figuration, lots of hand-crossing in a bumptious dialogue, and trills that gurgle like laughter. The suave sixth variation is the canon at the second, another hard job because, like the unison, it is difficult to clarify for the ear. This snakes along gracefully, however, with the gentle dissonance of the major second clearly audible but carried along by the steady, smooth rhythm. In variation 6, Bach also throws out a few harmonic hints of the emotional complexities to come.

Bach allocates the seventh variation to the gently rocking motion of the *giga*, a dance rhythm he liked well. He ends all but two of the dance suites with one, there using the French name of *gigue*—in English it's *jig*. A piping figure is notable; this section oozes a mock-rustic charm. The eighth variation is a toccata in two fast-moving parts, where scurrying figures seem to want to pull the music ahead; at the end of

both sections, Bach speeds up note values, increasing the impetus. By
now you may have guessed that the canon that concludes this group
is at the third, a sweetly euphonious interval. And the variation itself
does not disappoint, with its close counterpoint in the right hand, the
interweaving lines sounding almost Chopin-esque in their richness and
complexity. Listen, too, for the active expansion of the ground bass
theme in the left.

The tenth variation, described by Bach as a *fughetta*—a little
fugue—is the first variation where the composer flaunts his contrapuntal mastery openly. The tone of the solidly built section may be
pompous, but assuredly comical, and the mood jovial. The toccata
movement that follows, the most fine-boned of the *Goldbergs*, offers
an enormous contrast in texture. Delicate in rhythm and strangely
skittish, this study in two voices, so different in mood from the other
toccata variations, may foreshadow some of Beethoven's ethereal late
piano music. And variation 12, the canon at the fourth that rounds out
this fourth grouping of variations, opens with the ground bass theme
hammered out decisively by the left hand. But the canon itself is dense
and complex. It is an inverted one, meaning that the two canonic voices
move in opposite directions, one going up while the other goes down.
It sounds complex because it is; yet Bach's mastery is easy rather than
demanding, and his tone Olympian as he regally solves the technical
problem he sets himself, without struggling for meretricious effect.

Larger in scope, the next three variations bring a change in tone as
we approach the midpoint of the set. The thirteenth variation presents
the theme in an otherwordly guise. Moving slowly over a graceful
elaboration of the ground bass in the left hand, the right decorates the
theme with lavish sprays of notes that remind some of baroque flute
music, spurring the unofficial nickname of the "Flute Variation." The
toccata variation is another wild take on hand-crossing, trills, and running figuration that seems at once hilarious and ecstatic. It is also very
difficult to play. And with the fifteenth variation—the canon at the
fifth—we hear the unmistakable note of tragedy with the first appearance of the tonic minor key, and an emphatic slowing of the prevailing
tempos, which have so far been lively. At the end, the music seems to
float away in despair. Drenched in sorrow, the effect of this variation is

tremendous. Bach, the complete artist, refuses to exclude sorrow from this grand display of his skills.

Bach takes a marvelous imaginative leap to open the *Goldbergs'* second half. The sixteenth variation is in the form of a French overture, like those that open the second and fourth partitas, and, of course the partita known as the French Overture itself (see page 101). In the greatest possible contrast with the sorrowful mood and thin texture in which variation 15 ends, this opens with the fat chords, bustling scales, trills, and stately dotted rhythm characteristic of the form. In a sovereign display of wit, Bach allocates the second half of the variation to a sparkling little fugue, just as the form requires. While observing all the French overture's formal demands, he creates a tone of mock pomposity that is surely comic; yet this variation satisfies musically on its own terms. With this wonderful variation, the *Goldbergs* seem reborn, right in the middle. The swift toccata that is variation seventeen takes on the characteristics of a perpetual motion piece. There is a wild scramble of notes at the end of the second half of this difficult variation. The canon at the sixth that follows is another fantastic display of contrapuntal mastery that wears its learning lightly. This jaunty movement is notable for the tightness of the canonic entries that, stretto-like, pile thickly on top of each other.

Variation 19 (CD Track 14) is an urbane little dance movement in three voices. The ground bass theme is clear in the left hand, broken though it is into a hopping figure (beginning through 0:08), after which the steady stream of quicker notes take over the active role (0:10). Bach compresses the melody to a tight range of notes, always in the right hand. The slight clash of melodic notes as they are held over after the next has been struck (0:11 to 0:18) creates a syncopation that adds a light swing to the music. The second half, beginning at 0:42, follows the course set by the first. What is remarkable, though, is how far it is in every audible and imaginative way from the theme, yet how recognizable that theme is, too.

Further yet is variation 20 (CD Track 15), arguably the wildest toccata in the set. Here, the bass line and melodic outline move back and forth between the hands in detached notes, remote from the tender songfulness of the theme as originally presented. Trills and hand crossing are continual throughout this virtuosic variation; listen, too, as it whirls by for the little three-note figure that first appears at 0:02, then again and again as it seems to pull the music along, then the chain of scurrying triplets that starts at 0:15 and spins busily thereafter. In the second half (starting at 1:00), the hands toss the ground bass around almost frantically. The left hand bangs it out at 1:14, seeming to keep possession, but the right grabs it (1:19), before the left snatches a bit of it (1:26) back once more just before the end.

Variation 21 (CD Track 16) is the canon at the seventh, a highly expressive interval the composer loved and used skillfully. The second of three variations in G minor, the tone of this section is somber, per-haps tragic, forming the starkest contrast imaginable with the preceding number. Here, Bach adds chromatic intervals—sighing half-steps that add tonal shadings—to the bass line, which is in itself one of the most eloquent in the work. Note also the very close writing of the bass and the two canonic voices, made quite clear at 0:17, the canonic imitation of the trills at 0:22 and 0:24, and the cellolike beauty of the bass line throughout the second half, beginning at 1:09.

As the work progresses, the moods of the variations grow more disparate, a trend the next three variations bear out. The first of these (variation 22) is a contrapuntal display where the theme may be heard clearly, starting in the left hand, followed by four voices entering in close succession. The toccata variation is another wild one, with scur-rying figures interspersed with a giggly two-note figure. A canon at the octave, moving in suave dance rhythm, rounds out the group.

More critical attention goes to the twenty-fifth variation than any other. As should be: this remarkable movement, longest by far of the *Goldbergs,* and third in the minor key, must dominate the work and the sensitive listener's imagination. It has nicknames: "Crown of Thorns," referring to the agony it expresses; and the "Black Pearl," which sug-gests its exquisite beauty. The best way to get to know this extraor-dinary movement is simply to listen, with or without a score, not to rush it, and to let it make its points in its own good time, which, given a chance, it must.

But a few ideas on how to approach it may help. With its abrupt slowing—almost to a halt—of musical movement and consequent increase in length, Bach here changes utterly the mood, time frame, and message of his work. These he accomplishes by giving a rare tempo indication: adagio ("slowly"; variation 15 gets the only other tempo marking in the work). Bach also decorates the melody with the most lavish and febrile ornamentation. The composer then subjects everything—ground bass, melody, and ornamentation—to intensive chromatic treatment. The audible result is the constant sense that the musical elements are sighing, weeping, and struggling to stay up and moving. After the dying end of the first half, you may find yourself wondering if it has the strength to continue.

Formally, variation 25 takes the place a big, slow movement would occupy in a composition of the classical or romantic eras. From an aesthetic standpoint, Bach probably saw that the cheerfulness that dominates the work needed balancing with a outpouring that fully articulates the grief and weariness the preceding minor-key variations (15 and 21) seem in comparison only to suggest. And it is obviously worth considering Bach's purpose in giving the longest section of the *Goldberg Variations* over to these dark ruminations, coloring this whole, grand set—so much of which is brisk, funny, and joyous—a far deeper hue.

Picking up his burden, now much heavier, Bach follows the great slow movement effectively with a toccata variation in which the theme, stated in slow notes in a stately sarabande rhythm, moves from hand to hand, switching off with a brisk, running accompaniment. The final canon, at the unusual interval of the ninth, rounds out this most varied of all the variation trios. Here the theme, unaccompanied by a bass voice, leaps manically from hand to hand. Performers say its exposed writing is accident prone and more difficult than it looks.

In the final three variations, Bach breaks away from the regular pattern established over most of the work. Variations 28 and 29 are both toccata-like in their brilliance, but differ greatly in mood. The first is a trill-laden moment of purest ecstasy from which Beethoven clearly learned a great deal. Comedy returns for variation 29, which opens with an imitation of drumbeats, followed by a blizzard of detached notes and chords in wild rhythms that jump from one hand to the other, and back again. Variation 30—the last, but not the last word in Bach's musical universe—is called a *quodlibet*. This difficult-sounding Latin word means "a pastiche of popular tunes," in this case, "I've Not Been with You for So Long" and "Cabbage and Turnips," over the ground bass theme. (Bach loved to sing improvised takeoffs similar to this, injecting off-color lyrics, with family and other musicians at boozy social gatherings.) All this may astonish the nonprofessional musician, but melodies do follow conventional patterns, making it easy for the all-knowing Bach to hear one embedded in another. This comical conclusion is jovial in mood and Jovian in its rich, four-voiced counterpoint.

How to end a work of such breadth and grandeur? Bach does what may surprise the first-time listener: he repeats the sarabande in its original form from which the whole grand structure springs. The effect is simple and complex, of an ineffably sweet homecoming that also allows us to marvel at the distance we have traveled, and at the worlds of joy and sorrow the composer drew from the theme. Few variations sets end this way, with a literal repeat of the theme; though Bach's own Chaconne also concludes in a restatement of its own terrifying theme, altered slightly for climactic effect. To say the least, the trivial waltz on which the huge structure of Beethoven's *Diabelli Variations* is based lacks the nobility of Bach's sarabande, depriving Beethoven of the possibility of emulating Bach with his own ending. But Beethoven does pretty well, too, concluding his own colossal variation set—that greatest possible tribute to Bach's—with a minuet that is a celestial takeoff of the little waltz theme. Beethoven's debt to Bach has been acknowledged from the start, with the publisher—Diabelli himself—writing in his promotional text for the publication in 1823 of Beethoven's great work that it was entitled to "a place beside Sebastian Bach's famous masterpiece in the same form."[6] The comment also makes it clear that the *Goldbergs* were well known, at least among the Viennese musical elite of the early nineteenth century.

Bach wrote the *Goldbergs* with repeat marks at the end of every half of both iterations of the theme at the work's beginning and end, and for every half of each of the thirty variations. Many performers, such as Jenö Jandó on the CD that accompanies this book, play every repeat, resulting in a recording that takes nearly eighty minutes. Others, like Glenn Gould in the first of his two recordings of the piece, take none: his performance comes in, predictably, at about half as long, at 38:56.

Both players employ comparable tempos, on the brisk side. But the difference is, necessarily and obviously, considerable between two performances of such a work as the *Goldberg Variations*. Without repeats, it will always seem more headlong and fantastical, as the variations whirl by; whereas with repeats it is, inevitably, more deliberate and weighty by dint of a doubled performance time and having material repeated. One undeniable advantage to performances with the repeats taken, is that one gets to rehear and reconsider ideas that are appealing or strange.

But there is no right or wrong path. Nor is it disrespectful to Bach and his score to omit the repeats: Wanda Landowska, whom few would accuse of lack of reverence for the composer, skips the repeats, and comes up with a sort of da capo arrangements for variations 7 and 18, by repeating their opening phrases at the end for emphasis; her idea works very well. In his second recording of the work, made in 1982, Glenn Gould employs more moderate tempos than in his daring, dashing 1955 version; he also takes thirteen repeats, yielding a traversal that is thoughtful, leisurely, and about thirteen minutes longer.

One final consideration about recordings concerns the edition performed. Bach's own printed copy of the *Goldbergs* was discovered in Strasbourg, France, in 1975, with the composer's own editorial markings in red ink. As one might expect, these directions, many of which show how Bach wanted ornamentation rendered, are of enormous significance and interest.[7] But of course recordings from before the early 1980s, including some of the best, were made without the benefit of these discoveries. So don't be surprised by differences between older and more recent recordings, and don't be afraid of owning several. At all events, the *Goldbergs* are durable enough to support many approaches.

The Works for Organ

ecause of the similarity in the names of many of the organ works, we are giving their BWV numbers, from a listing of all Bach's works, as an aid to their identification and to prevent confusion.

Bach's greatest fame in his own lifetime was probably as an organist, for which his skill was accorded the highest respect and praise. He composed most of his works for organ primarily for his own performance, but also for use in testing organs he was hired to inspect. One of his main sources of income was as an expert consultant on the construction of new organs, and the rebuilding and repair of old instruments. From his eighteenth year (which testifies to an ability that ripened very early) almost until his death, Bach traveled to German towns to inspect organs and write reports with his findings on their conditions and recommendations for improvement. The list of towns and cities he visited on such business is long, and very likely incomplete, as his every activity was not chronicled. But this very interesting aspect of Bach's career shows yet another side to a man whose compositions stand as great intellectual and spiritual testaments, who was also an expert at the highest level in the most complex of all musical instruments in design and mechanics. The survey format unfortunately permits only a quick look into this important category of Bach's work.

The German towns and noble families that possessed organs generally took great pride in their instruments and tried to take care of them, which was why Bach was hired to perform his inspections. Sometimes the instruments needed repair after damage or periods of neglect; at others, municipalities or princes, such as Bach's boss in Weimar, wanted to enlarge the organ in his chapel. The composer tested organs by playing his own works on them.

The organ, which dates back to classical antiquity, consists in its most basic form of a keyboard, a supply of forced air, pipes of different sizes tuned to different pitches, and a mechanism that moves the forced air into the pipes that are intended to sound, while stopping air from going to all the others. In practice, organs often have more than one keyboard—like a two-manual harpsichord—and pedals operated by the player's feet, producing the organ's earth-shaking low notes. Organ builders over the centuries also began to add a wide variety of *stops,* pipes of different woods and metals and of different lengths, that gave new kinds of timbres to the instrument; thus, some stops might suggest the sound of woodwinds; and others, brass instruments.

The organ has been called "king of instruments"; indeed, hearing a fine one, well played, is an extraordinary experience, physically as well as aesthetically. The organs of Bach's time were built and improved during a golden age of organ construction and playing. Big organs were only found in churches and the private chapels of princes; small organs in homes were exceedingly rare. The organ was, therefore, associated with ceremony and high occasion, from Sunday services to celebrations of events in the lives of ruling families. Bach played his works for organ in churches and royal chapels, before, during, and after such ceremonies. Although the bulk his works for organ are chorale preludes, based on Lutheran hymns, and the purely musical forms like the preludes, toccatas, and fugues are written in the secular manner of German, French, and Italian models, Bach would have played both types of works in the course of a Sunday performance. The hymn-based pieces accompanied services, whereas the toccatas, preludes, and fugue served as musical postludes, keeping the interested (many, one imagines) in church to hear Bach play.

The division of his organ music into sacred and secular is, therefore, more a convenience of definition for an overview like this than a distinction Bach is likely to have observed. As another example of the congruence in the composer's work of secular and sacred forms for this instrument, the first, second, and fourth volumes of his *Clavier-Übung* are for harpsichord and all incontestably secular. Volume 3, for organ, is an encyclopedic assembly, mostly but not exclusively of chorale preludes—the settings of hymn melodies—framed by a massive prelude and a fugue in E-flat major, nicknamed the "St. Anne," and nearly always performed together, without reference to rest of the set. To Bach, therefore, the *Clavier-Übung* was wide enough to hold all kinds of musical concepts, and even the chiefly "sacred" third volume is not made up entirely of church music.

The Lutheran hymns on which Bach based his pieces for church services, most of which are brief and called chorale preludes, follow a pattern of rising and falling tension. In the Lutheran churches of North German communities, organists, including giants such as Sweelinck, Pachelbel, and Bach's likely teacher, the great Dietrich Buxtehude, played elaborations of these sturdy melodies as preludes and interludes in services; Bach brought this form of composition to its highest point. To the composer's fertile mind, each suggested a number of treatments, some of which he probably improvised in church, then wrote down afterwards. It will not surprise those who have grasped the composer's character and style to learn that Bach was so daring in his adaptations of the chorales that he was reprimanded by the authorities in Arnstadt for introducing "too many strange tones"[1]—expressive and unusual harmonies that startled the congregation, accustomed to hearing their hymns played plainly. But he composed hundreds of chorale preludes on the hymn melodies.

In a typical chorale prelude, such as "Von Himmel hoch, da komm' ich her," BWV 738—"From Heaven on high I come," a Christmas chorale by Martin Luther, the chorale melody emerges in long, clear notes from a welter of ornamentation, set in a forceful rhythmic pattern. Bach's ornamentation is never merely decorative but always rigorously polyphonic, often in various types of canonic imitation. In another of the several chorale preludes he composed to the same chorale, this one with the BWV listing of 701, the melody may be treated as the basis for a *fughetta*—a short fugue. The extraordinary sophistication and weightlessness of its counterpoint makes this joyful little essay seem a work from later in the composer's career. It's also identical in subject and similar in tone to Bach's Canonic Variations on *Von Himmel hoch*—see page **XXX** for more on this dizzying masterwork. But even more important to the listener than Bach's ironclad contrapuntal technique is the expressive goal he meets again and again in these brilliant short works, adding to the straightforward sincerity of the chorale tunes an affect that always enhances, embroiders, and deepens the meaning of text.

Two collections of works for organ stand as the best known of the collections, the homogeneous *Orgelbüchlein*—the "Little Organ Book"—and the more diverse *Clavier-Übung III*. The first collection, in two volumes, dates from Bach's years in Weimar and Cöthen, the early phase of his artistic maturity. He arranged these relatively brief settings of hymn tunes into groups connected with the holidays when the chorales—the hymns—were sung by the congregation, and when he played his settings: Advent, Christmas, New Year, Purification, Passiontide, Easter, Pentecost, and a final group of ten, linked to the Ten Commandments, under the rubric "Faith."

These sublime works are closely tied to their function as preludes to and interludes during a church service. They show Bach both practical and profound, as he meditates musically on the meanings of the texts to the hymns that he and the congregations grew up with and knew by heart. These are works that that contemporary, secular listeners must try to take on their own terms, without questioning the faith of their composer and his audience of fellow believers. At all events, they are majestic creations that stand on their own, reflecting the joy, pain, and doubt of human existence.

The *Clavier-Übung III,* published in 1739, contains works of great diversity, from a colossal six-part arrangement of the hymn "Aus tiefer not" ("Out of the deep I cry to thee") to four wiry but gorgeous *duetti,* which are essentially two-part inventions for organ. In this, probably his greatest collection for the organ, Bach presents a triumphant lesson in how to compose for the instrument in a wide range of styles.

More than two hundred chorale preludes survive under Bach's name. Others are terribly and almost certainly lost; some of those long attributed to him now seem doubtful to Bach scholars. The two volumes of the *Orgelbüchlein* and a grouping known as the "Neumeister collection" after an obscure eighteenth-century German musician whose handwriting the preludes are in, are the largest groups. It's now considered uncertain whether any of the Neumesiter pieces are by Bach.

Other groupings are known as the *Schübler Chorales,* the Kirnbirger Collection, and "The Eighteen" have been under longer critical and academic scrutiny, and so are more convincingly divided into works clearly in Bach's styles over his long career and those that now appear doubtful in their early attributions to him. And another fifty-one chorale preludes are independent of any collections or groupings.

Six works fall into the category of chorale variations, more extended studies on chorale themes. Five of these, generally referred to as "partitas," appear to be early works. They have nothing to do with the later partitas for harpsichord, which are, of course, integrated suites of dance pieces, and it's not even clear that Bach himself called them by that name. In the score, each variation, of which there are six to eleven per set, is called a "partita." Although unsophisticated in comparison to Bach's later organ works, they do have a distinct charm, as the earnest young composer develops his own style.

The sixth set is the late, great "Canonic Variations on *Von Himmel hoch,*" one of the composer's most majestic contrapuntal exercises. According to Lorenz Mizler, writer of an obituary of the composer that appeared in 1754, Bach wrote the piece in 1747 on his admission to the Leipzig Society for the Musical Sciences.[2] As with the *Goldberg Variations,* this was the sort of challenge Bach welcomed, a rigorous contrapuntal working out of a musical idea, rather than a mere decoration of a theme. The piece is in its way more challenging for the listener, as well, in its exclusive focus on canon, without the toccatas and character pieces that make up the *Goldbergs.* The chorale theme, "Von Himmel hoch, da komm' ich her" (From Heaven high came I here) is the same Christmas hymn that Bach had set in chorale prelude form at least four times previously, two of which are discussed above. As in the *Goldberg Variations,* Bach designs these canons to contrast with one another as to show his own skills, which by this late point in his career were a wonder of the musical world.

Unlike his other important variations, the melody is never stated independently, the work beginning with the first variation, a canon, at the octave, and the chorale theme in the bass. The second variation, at the fifth, with the theme again played by the pedal and the canon, worked out freely on the keyboard. The third variation is a cheerful canon at the seventh with the introduction of a complementary melody; and the fourth presents the tune-stretched-out in augmentation. The fifth variation is the most elaborate and strange, presenting the theme in reverse at the sixth, then the third, the second, the ninth, and finally in diminution, all in quick succession. The theme rings out clearly but the accompanying lines do indeed seem to be running backward. It may sound difficult, and this is hardly Bach's most straightforward piece, but it exudes throughout an unmistakable and bracing joy in mastery. It should also come as no surprise that the Canonic Variations do reward repeated listening and patience, as the ear begins to disentangle its complex patterns. In homage to the work, Stravinsky made a rarely heard transcription of it for orchestra.

Bach's "secular" organ works—those without overt religious associations—are many and varied. Some stand among his greatest and most famous compositions, while others are less known and less highly regarded. The Toccata and Fugue in D Minor, BWV 565, has long been a popular favorite. But readers who know and love it for its spooky drama need to and sit down and take a deep breath, because there's bad news: many experts now find it atypically simple in too many ways and question its attribution to Bach. Geck refers to its "paucity of contrapuntal effects"[3]; and Williams to its "limited harmonic vocabulary."[4] Even Wolff, who doesn't openly question its authorship, calls it "structurally undisciplined and unmastered."[5] The piece may be a transcription of a work for solo violin, or by another, later composer entirely. The least any realistic music lover who has listened extensively to Bach can observe is that it does lack his normal intellectual focus and rigorous structural approach.

Bach's claim to the other Toccata and Fugue in D minor, the so-called "Dorian," is not in question, though. The stern opening section, a dialogue of idiomatic organ writing is as impressive as it could be as well as intellectually cohesive in a way that the questionable BWV 565 is not, for all its flash. The long fugue, based on a serious subject, is daring harmonically, looking ahead in places to Bach's final contrapuntal masterwork, *The Art of Fugue*. The closing phrases look back to the opening of this magnificent work.

The Toccata, Adagio, and Fugue in C major, BWV 564 is a spacious and impressive suite in three movements, as the title suggests. The work opens with a long and exciting passage, filled with scale work that sounds as though it began as an improvisation. This leads to a grand main section in a steadier rhythm and more relaxed mood; Bach moves freely and calmly from key to key. Grandeur and excitement merge in the closing bars. The middle movement is a beautiful Italian concerto-like movement, with a melody over a rocking accompaniment that moves into an even slower passage, in which Bach explores some daring harmonic territory. The fugue, on a short-winded, even chirpy subject that Bach develops into a structure of unexpected grandeur. This fine work has a breadth, good humor, and tranquility all its own. Some readers may know the transcription of the work for piano by the early twentieth-century pianist and composer Ferrucio Busoni that Vladimir Horowitz played in his famous return to the recital stage in 1965.

The huge Toccata and Fugue in F major, BWV 540, is one of Bach's unquestioned masterpieces for organ. The opening section is remarkable for its enormous dimensions and force, as well as for the economy of material Bach employs in building a structure so vast and tight. These few ideas—a long-held pedal point, busy hand figuration typical of a toccata, and a few chords, dramatically stated and harmonized—form the entire body of this astonishing ten-page, ten-minute work; the composer's handling of his material is stunning, and the entire movement is an outburst of epic energy from start to finish. The work opens with perpetual-motion figuration for the hands over a long-held (fifty-four bars!) F in the pedal. After the hands toss the rapid material around, the feet take over, in an extraordinary display of pedal virtuosity. A brief chord sequence intervenes, after which Bach repeats the entire long opening sequence in C major. This finally breaks into furious chords in another high-energy rhythmic incarnation. Bach tosses these ideas back and forth to the end; despite the changes of pattern, the musical flow is continuous and volcanic. The four-voice fugue, based on two subjects, the first a stirring one mostly in long notes with a chromatic element, the second with a stronger rhythmic profile, is another tremendous discharge of power. As the fugue progresses, its rolling force seems to gain in grace and fluidity—there are moments that seem almost danceable—and lyricism, as well. Some have proposed that subtle stylistic differences suggest different dates of composition for this pair; but even if true, they seem flawlessly matched and contrasted.

Even in an oeuvre as formidable as Bach's the Prelude and Fugue in E-flat major, BWV 552, is a magnificent achievement, and one of his greatest instrumental compositions. As noted, the two elements of this pair stand separately as the mighty portals to the third volume of the *Clavier-Übung,* the Prelude as its opening work, and the fugue as its concluding one, but the two are always paired in performance. They are sometimes known by the irrelevant nickname "St. Anne," tacked on by English listeners because of the resemblance of one of the fugue subjects to an Anglican hymn. The entire work, which Bach composed in his full maturity, is at the highest level from every conceivable perspective. These include, but are hardly limited to, its structure, which is at once broad and strict; its counterpoint, remarkable even for Bach; and its musical style, which is a glorious amalgam and summation of the many national influences and polyphonic styles the composer mastered.

The Prelude, in which Bach deploys three contrasting ideas, opens with a statement in a noble rhythmic figure reminiscent of a French overture but not as set in its ways as that rigid style of writing. This theme has an easier swing, if just as much grandeur. The second thematic idea consists of a chordal group, also easy in its elegant rhythmic swing and also noble in character. The first idea returns; then the third appears, in faster notes with a more intense motion that sets it apart from the other two themes. Bach then reprises the first theme, then the second, then the third, in different keys, showing each in new and different shadings. To conclude his mammoth structure emphatically and convincingly, the composer brings back the opening idea, now radiant in its unforced majesty. The structure of this movement is singular, conceived by the composer to suit the splendor of his ideas and the room they needed for development; closer, experts think, to a concerto movement than that of an overture, but in any case the noblest of hybrids.

Bach conceived the fugue, like the Prelude, in three distinct parts, so it's referred to as a *compound fugue.* The opening section, on a long, winding subject, has an old-fashioned flavor that covers a narrow range and seems the musical equivalent of a glorious sunrise; the second theme is in a more flowing time signature but a similar and complementary pattern. With the third, Bach changes meter, cutting loose with a running subject in the long, loping 12/8 beat he loved. In some ways the structure of the fugue recalls some of the other great E-flat major fugues of Bach we've heard, notably that from Book I of *The Well-Tempered Clavier,* and the one in the middle of the Prelude, Fugue, and Allegro, BWV 998; but it's the biggest and grandest of all, a kind of summing-up of his ideas about what a fugue in E-flat major should say. There's no disagreement or carping about this pair; one writer calls the fugue "the height of perfection;"[6] another describes its ending, flat-out, as "the grandest . . . to any fugue in music."[7] The twenty-minutes playing time shown on a CD sleeve says little about the worlds of radiant tone and thought it holds.

The Passacaglia and Fugue in C minor (CD Tracks 17 and 18), are deservedly well known and revered. They are paired works; the first, a tight set of twenty variations on a ground bass, the stern theme for which is stated at the outset by the pedal. A *passacaglia* is a variation form on a ground bass theme that appears to have originated as a dance in Spain, and worked its way north, like so many of the forms used by Bach and others. As every commentator has to note, a passacaglia is impossible to tell apart from a chaconne; all inevitably point out as other examples Bach's own Chaconne for solo violin, Dido's great aria "When I am laid in earth" from Purcell's *Dido and Aeneas,* Beethoven's Thirty-two Variations in C Minor, the last movement of Brahms's Symphony No. 4 in E Minor, and the last movement of Britten's String Quartet No. 2 in C Major. Anyone who listens to all of these in one sitting may be crazy, or will be afterward; but she or he will readily perceive the tight structure they all share, the steely grip of the form over the musical expression. As noted on page 114, Bach's *Goldberg Variations* are a close relative, a longer set built on a longer theme that is also underpinned by a ground bass, as well; it's just as organized as these but its proportions are far bigger, and its tone far more upbeat. Bach's own Chaconne, tremendous and terrifying, is the closest relative to these dark-hued variations.

Both the Chaconne and the *Goldbergs* come from the composer's maturity, however. The sonatas and partitas for solo violin, which contain the Chaconne, date to his Weimar years, 1720 or 1721; the *Goldbergs* of course came much later, published by the composer in 1741. Bach appears to have composed the Passacaglia and Fugue not long after 1705 under the influence of Buxtehude, the brilliant composer and organist he visited, heard, and probably studied with that year. Thus the Passacaglia and Fugue date from Bach's early twenties, an astonishingly mature work in every way for the young composer, and probably his greatest composition to that point.

The structure of the Passacaglia is simple and easy to follow. As noted, the theme is stated in the pedals at the beginning, and Bach repeats its notes in every variation, forming a clearly audible musical bedrock. Listen to its fearful power even in its barest form (CD Track 17) at the beginning as it rises, then gravely sinks.

The twenty variations that follow are connected but clearly demarcated by differences in their character and texture. These are easily noted, but it probably makes more sense for the first-time listener to let the inexorable, relentless power of the music carry him or her than to worry about counting off episodes and timings.

But for those who always need to know where they are, here are a few landmarks: the first variation, at 0:38, and the second, at 1:14, both add moaning accompaniments to the theme. The fourth, at 2:20, offers a new rising decoration in a short-short-long rhythm; the fifth (2:50) turns the ornament upside down, making it fall. The eighth variation (4:26) has passagework that twists and turns powerfully in opposite directions. With the ninth variation (4:57), Bach breaks the theme itself and his decoration of it into an open figuration. The tenth variation (5:27) places the theme into chords in the left hand and pedal, with arching sixteenth-note scales and figures in the right. The eleventh (5:59) places the theme into relief in the right hand, with figuration below and the pedal silent. Variation 14 (7:28) puts it into arpeggios, again without with the pedal, whereas 15 (7:53) breaks it into a light, memorable pattern of arpeggios that rise from deep in the left hand high up the keyboard; again, the pedals stay quiet. The furious, racing triplets of the seventeenth variation at 8:57 are impossible to miss, as are the ever-thickening textures and blistering power of the nineteenth and twentieth, at 9:59 and 10:29, respectively.

The Fugue (CD Track 18), which is connected with the Passacaglia and follows it without pause, forms its massive, somber pendant. Bach intended that the works be played together; they require each other aesthetically, forming a single, potent unit. This triple (three-subject) fugue is like the Passacaglia, very tightly organized and immensely powerful from start to finish. Bach presents the first theme, based on that of the Passacaglia but shortened, and the second, in steady, powerful repeated notes, together right at the start. The third, in faster-moving notes, enters at 0:19. (The attentive may note that the first and second themes have also entered again, just before.) From there on, Bach combines the three subjects in many complex ways, so this is simply to help the newbie identify them. It may be worth listening for the lightening of texture and move into less gloomy tonal region beginning at 1:41, and a new phase of darker intensity Bach initiates at 4:45. As he approaches the final moments, the juggernaut he has unleashed seems almost out of control: note the powerful stretto sequences at 6:45, where the fragments of the second and third subjects seem to be straining at the reins. Bach finally halts them masterfully with the tremendous chord from 7:01 to 7:10; then a pause, before he cuts loose the avalanche to the end.

These are hardly Bach's only worthwhile organ works. There are dozens of preludes, fantasias, and fugues that repay knowledge and study. Of particular beauty and well worth the listening are the six Trio Sonatas, BWV 525 to 530, urbane and suave secular pieces from about 1730. *Trio* refers to the three polyphonic lines in each of these sonatas. Some may have originated as chamber sonatas for flute, violin, and harpsichord; some wound up transcribed for that ensemble. And they sound fine that way, too.

Bach and His Followers

eaders who know the keyboard repertory even a little are probably aware of Bach's enormous influence on many of the masters who followed. This composer's part writing echoes through the piano music of Haydn, Mozart, Beethoven, Mendelssohn, Chopin, Schumann, Brahms, and Schoenberg, not necessarily in the application of strict counterpoint, but in the discipline of thinking in polyphonic lines. (The influence is not universal, however. Schubert didn't think polyphonically. Liszt was a student and player of Bach, but his piano sound was based on the tonal capabilities of the instrument, as was Ravel's. Debussy revered Bach but purposely steered his music away from existing forms and sounds.)

What drew the composers for keyboard who followed Bach to study him and to metabolize his style is not only the polyphonic mastery, impressed by it though they clearly were. It was the way Bach merged the intellectual rigor of counterpoint with the furious, earthy energy of dance, all the while expressing a range of emotion that's as wide as it is deep.

It's the completeness of Bach's spirit—his humanity as well as his mystical fervor and enormous intellect—that draws us to him. Musicians may admire his skill, seeing the brilliance of his compositional strategies. The average, music-loving listener may have a sense of what's going on structurally without being able to name it. But all stand equal before Bach's emotional power, be it joy, sorrow, ecstasy, or fury finding expression with the shocking clarity of his genius.

And the generations of pianists, teachers, and piano students know it, too. Difficult as this composer's music is to master (and it is hard to learn, as any player can attest), the joy of learning it is enormous. Even at its simplest, Bach's music is startlingly complex. The two-part Inventions, for example, are still tricky, painfully slow in the mastering, and easy to lose if one doesn't play them regularly and often. Yet for all its difficulties, studying Bach as a player is one of the greatest and most joyful experiences a music lover can have. It's not just hitting the right notes in the right order that challenges and thrills, it's to feel in the hands the astonishing mix of cerebral polyphony and surging, choreographically expressed passion that makes Bach so rewarding, even for the amateur.

So, in one sense, students of Bach can feel and know what better men and women before have felt and known, and count themselves in the fine company of the amateurs and teachers; the keyboard players fair, good, and great; and the mighty ones who have humbly and proudly counted themselves among Bach's followers.

Notes

Chapter 1

1. William Elders, book jacket and 146.
2. Quoted in Elders, 133.
3. Judith Robison, notes to *The Art of Igor Kipnis, Volume 2*.
4. Igor Kipnis, introduction to *The Art of Igor Kipnis, Volume 2*.
5. Peter Williams, *J. S. Bach: A Life in Music*, 255.

Chapter 2

1. Wolff, 525–34.
2. Quoted in Wolff, 427.

Chapter 4

1. Rosen, *Critical Entertainments*, 35.

Chapter 5

1. Williams, *J. S. Bach: A Life in Music*, 131.
2. Rudolf Steglich, preface to *Französische Suiten*, iv.
3. Walther Deinhard, preface to Bach, *Englische Suiten*, xi.
4. Colin Tilney, "Suggestions for Performance" in Bach, *Englische Suiten*, xv.
5. Rudolf Steglich, preface to Bach, *Französische Suiten,* iv.
6. *The Oxford Dictionary of Music*, 524.

Chapter 6

1. Rosen, *Critical Entertainments,* 37.
2. Landowska, *Landowska on Music*, 148.
3. Ledbetter, 41.
4. Williams, *J. S. Bach: A Life in Music*, 144.
5. Wolff, 235.
6. Ledbetter, 116.

7. Rosen, *The Romantic Generation,* 359.
8. Kirkpatrick, 11.
9. Engels, *Bach's Well-Tempered Clavier,* 22.
10. Landowska, *Landowska on Music,* 242–43.
11. Ledbetter, 176.
12. Ibid., 174.
13. Engels, 108.
14. Ledbetter, 198.
15. Landowska, *Landowska on Music,* 194–95.

Chapter 7

1. Rosen, *Critical Entertainments,* 38.
2. Tovey, *Forty-Eight Preludes and Fugues,* 5.
3. Landowska, *Landowska on Music,* 197.
4. Ibid., 197
5. Ibid., 199.
6. Ledbetter, 278–81.
7. Tovey, *Forty-Eight Preludes and Fugues,* 25.
8. Ledbetter, 315–16.

Chapter 8

1. Landowska, liner notes to *Legendary Performers: Landowska,* 17.
2. Friskin and Freundlich, 56.
3. Williams, *J. S. Bach: A Life in Music,* 230.

Chapter 9

1. Wolff, 74.
2. Geck, 488–92.

Chapter 10

1. Quoted in Mellers, 262.
2. Ibid., 263
3. Wolff, 377.
4. Mellers, 263.
5. Landowska, *Landowska on Music,* 215.
6. Quoted in Tovey, *Chamber Music,* 124.
7. Bach, *Goldberg Variations,* Rudolf Steglich, ed., vii and 115.

Chapter 11

1. Wolff, 85.
2. Williams, *The Organ Music of J. S. Bach,* 512–24.
3. Geck, 56.
4. Williams, *The Organ Music of J. S. Bach,* 157.
5. Wolff, 169.
6. Geck, 496.
7. Williams, *The Organ Music of J. S. Bach,* 140.

Selected Bibliography

Bach, J. S. *Chromatische Fantasie und Fuge*. Mainz: Wiener Urtext Edition, Schott/Universal Edition, 1999.

————. *Englische Suiten*. Mainz: Wiener Urtext Edition, Schott/Universal Edition, 1998.

————. *Französische Suiten*. G. Henle Verlag, 1972.

————. *Inventionien und Sinfonien*. Kassel: Bärenreiter-Verlag, 1972.

————. *Italienisches Konzert, Französische Ouverture, Vier Duette, Goldberg-Variationen*. G. Henle Verlag, 1975. Revision, 1979.

————. *Organ Music, the Bach-Gesellschaft Edition*. Mineola, N.Y.: Dover Publications, 1970.

————. *Sechs Partiten*. G. Henle Verlag, 1970. Revision 1979.

————. *Toccatas, Fantasias, Passacaglia and Other Works for Organ From the Bach-Gesellschaft Edition*. New York: Dover Publications, 1987.

————. *Toccaten*. Mainz: Wiener Urtext Edition, Schott/Universal Edition, 2000.

————. *Das Wohltemperierte Klavier I*. Mainz: Wiener Urtext Edition, Schott/Universal Edition, 1977. Revision, 2001.

————. *Das Wohltemperierte Klavier II*. Mainz: Wiener Urtext Edition, Schott/Universal Edition, 1983. Revision, 2001.

Boulez, Pierre. *Orientations*. Translated by Martin Cooper. Cambridge, MA: Harvard University Press, 1986.

Duffin, Ross. *How Equal Temperament Ruined Harmony (and Why You Should Care)*. New York: W. W. Norton and Co., 2007.

Elders, William. *Composers of the Low Countries*. Translated by Graham Dixon. Oxford: Oxford University Press, 1991.

Engels, Marjorie Wornell. *Bach's Well-Tempered Clavier: An Exploration of the 48 Preludes and Fugues*. Jefferson, NC: McFarland and Co., 2006.

Friskin, James, and Irwin Freundlich. *Music for the Piano*. New York: Dover Publications, 1973.

Geck, Martin. *Bach: Life and Work*. Translated by John Hargraves. Orlando, FL: Harcourt Books, 2006.

Isacoff, Stuart. *Temperament: How Music Became a Battleground for the Great Minds of Western Civilization*. New York: Vintage Books, 2003.

Kennedy, Michael, ed. *The Oxford Dictionary of Music.* 2nd ed. Oxford: Oxford University Press, 1994.

Kipnis, Igor, harpsichord and clavichord. *The Art of Igor Kipnis, Vol. 2: Harpsichord and Clavichord Music of England, Germany, and Austria.* Columbia Records, M3X32325 (3 vinyl records). Original sound recordings made by CBS, Inc. ℗ 1973.

Kirkpatrick, Ralph. *Interpreting Bach's Well-Tempered Clavier.* New Haven, CT: Yale University Press, 1984.

Landowska, Wanda. *Landowska on Music.* Collected, edited, and translated by Denise Restout and Robert Hawkins. New York: Stein and Day, 1964.

————, piano. *Legendary Performers: Landowska.* BMG 09026-60919-2. ℗ 1992, BMG Music TMK(s) ® G.E. Co., USA & BMG Music (2 compact discs). (Includes J. S. Bach's *Goldberg Variations,* Two- and Three-Part Inventions, and Partita No. 2.)

Ledbetter, David. *Bach's Well-tempered Clavier: The 48 Preludes and Fugues.* New Haven, CT: Yale University Press, 2002.

Libbey, Ted. *The NPR Listener's Encyclopedia of Classical Music.* New York: Workman Publishing, 2006.

Mellers, Wilfrid. *Bach and the Dance of God.* London: Faber and Faber, 1980. Republished by Travis and Emery, 2007.

Rosen, Charles. *Critical Entertainments: Music Old and New.* Cambridge, MA: Harvard University Press, 2000.

————. *Piano Notes: The World of the Pianist.* New York: Free Press, 2002.

————. *The Romantic Generation.* Cambridge, MA: Harvard University Press, 1995.

Tovey, Donald Francis. *Chamber Music.* Oxford: Oxford University Press, 1944. 8th edition, 1989.

————, ed. Preface, *Forty-Eight Preludes and Fugues by J. S. Bach, Book II.* New York: Oxford University Press, 1924.

Williams, Peter. *J. S. Bach: A Life in Music.* Cambridge: Cambridge University Press, 2007.

————. *The Organ Music of J. S. Bach.* 2nd ed. Cambridge: Cambridge University Press, 2003.

Wolff, Christoph. *Johann Sebastian Bach: The Learned Musician.* New York: W. W. Norton and Co., 2000.

CD Track Listing

1. Two-Part Invention No. 8 in F Major, BWV 779 (1:13)
   Wolfgang Rübsam, piano
   From Naxos CD 8.55096

2. Sinfonia in F Minor, BWV 795 (3:52)
   Wolfgang Rübsam, piano
   From Naxos CD 8.55096

3. French Suite No. 5 in G Major, BWV 816: Loure (2:56)
   Wolfgang Rübsam, piano
   From Naxos CD 8.550710

4. English Suite No. 6 in D Minor, BWV 811: Gavotte I and II (5:08)
   Wolfgang Rübsam, piano
   From Naxos CD 8.553013

5. *The Well-Tempered Clavier*, Book I: Prelude No. 2 in C Minor, BWV 847 (1:41)
   Luc Beauséjour, harpsichord
   From Naxos CD 8.557625

6. *The Well-Tempered Clavier*, Book I: Fugue No. 2 in C Minor, BWV 847 (1:40)
   Luc Beauséjour, harpsichord
   From Naxos CD 8.557625

7. *The Well-Tempered Clavier*, Book II: Prelude and Fugue No. 11 in F Major, BWV 880 (4:46)
   Jenö Jandö, piano
   From Naxos CD 8.550970

8. Partita No. 4 in D Major, BWV 828: Overture (6:40)
Wolfgang Rübsam, piano
From Naxos CD 8.550693

9. Partita No. 4 in D Major, BWV 828: Gigue (3:46)
Wolfgang Rübsam, piano
From Naxos CD 8.550693

10. Italian Concerto, BWV 971: Allegro (3:50)
János Sebestyén, piano
From Naxos CD 8.550571

11. Italian Concerto, BWV 971: Andante (5:08)
János Sebestyén, piano
From Naxos CD 8.550571

12. Italian Concerto, BWV 971: Presto (3:59)
János Sebestyén, piano
From Naxos CD 8.550571

13. *Goldberg Variations*, BWV 988: Aria (3:57)
Jenö Jandö, piano
From Naxos CD 8.557268

14. *Goldberg Variations*, BWV 988: Variation 20 (1:29)
Jenö Jandö, piano
From Naxos CD 8.557268

15. *Goldberg Variations*, BWV 988: Variation 21 (2:05)
Jenö Jandö, piano
From Naxos CD 8.557268

16. *Goldberg Variations*, BWV 988: Variation 22 (2:24)
Jenö Jandö, piano
From Naxos CD 8.557268

17. Passacaglia and Fugue in C Minor, BWV 582: Passacaglia (11:13)
Wolfgang Rübsam, organ
From Naxos CD 8.553859

18. Passacaglia and Fugue in C Minor, BWV 582: Fugue (8:20)
Wolfgang Rübsam, organ
From Naxos CD 8.553859

UNLOCKING THE MASTERS

The highly acclaimed Unlocking the Masters series brings readers into the world of the greatest composers and their music. All books come with CDs that have tracks taken from the world's foremost libraries of recorded classics, bringing the music to life.

"With infectious enthusiasm and keen insight, the Unlocking the Masters series succeeds in opening our eyes, ears, hearts, and minds to the great composers." – *Strings*

...OVEN'S SYMPHONIES:
...TENER'S GUIDE
...n Bell Young
...2.95 • 978-1-57467-169-8 • HL00331951

...MS: A LISTENER'S GUIDE
...n Bell Young
...2.95 • 978-1-57467-171-1• HL00331974

...IN: A LISTENER'S GUIDE TO THE
...ER OF THE PIANO
...tor Lederer
...2.95 • 978-1-57467-148-3 • HL00331699

...SSY: THE QUIET REVOLUTIONARY
...tor Lederer
...2.95 • 978-1-57467-153-7 • HL00331743

...ÁK: ROMANTIC MUSIC'S
...VERSATILE GENIUS
...vid Hurwitz
...7.95 • 978-1-57467-107-0 • HL00331662

...REAT INSTRUMENTAL WORKS
...Owen Lee
...7.95 • 978-1-57467-117-9 • HL00331672

...RING HAYDN: A LISTENER'S GUIDE
...USIC'S BOLDEST INNOVATOR
...vid Hurwitz
...7.95 • 978-1-57467-116-2 • HL00331671

...A LISTENER'S GUIDE
...n Bell Young
...2.99 • 978-1-57467-170-4 • HL00331952

...AHLER SYMPHONIES:
...WNER'S MANUAL
...vid Hurwitz
...2.95 • 978-1-57467-099-8 • HL00331650

...'S FIRST MASTER: THE MUSICAL
...AS OF CLAUDIO MONTEVERDI
...rk Ringer
...9.95 • 978-1-57467-110-0 • HL00331665

GETTING THE MOST OUT OF MOZART:
THE VOCAL WORKS
by David Hurwitz
US $22.95 • 978-1-57467-106-3 • HL00331661

GETTING THE MOST OUT OF MOZART:
THE INSTRUMENTAL WORKS
by David Hurwitz
US $22.95 • 978-1-57467-096-7 • HL00331648

PUCCINI: A LISTENER'S GUIDE
by John Bell Young
US $22.95 • 978-1-57467-172-8 • HL00331975

SHOSTAKOVICH SYMPHONIES AND CONCERTOS:
AN OWNER'S MANUAL
by David Hurwitz
US $22.95 • 978-1-57467-131-5 • HL00331692

SIBELIUS, THE ORCHESTRAL WORKS:
AN OWNER'S MANUAL
by David Hurwitz
US $27.95 • 978-1-57467-149-0 • HL00331735

TCHAIKOVSKY: A LISTENER'S GUIDE
by Daniel Felsenfeld
US $27.95 • 978-1-57467-134-6 • HL00331697

DECODING WAGNER: AN INVITATION TO HIS
WORLD OF MUSIC DRAMA
by Thomas May
US $27.95 • 978-1-57467-097-4 • HL00331649

AMADEUS PRESS

www.amadeuspress.com
Prices and availability subject to change
without notice.